Bee Busy Coloring

ISBN: 9798994484821

For more creations, coloring pages, and upcoming books, visit:

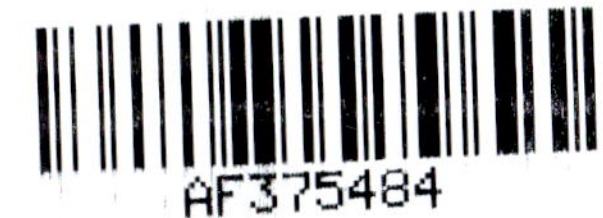

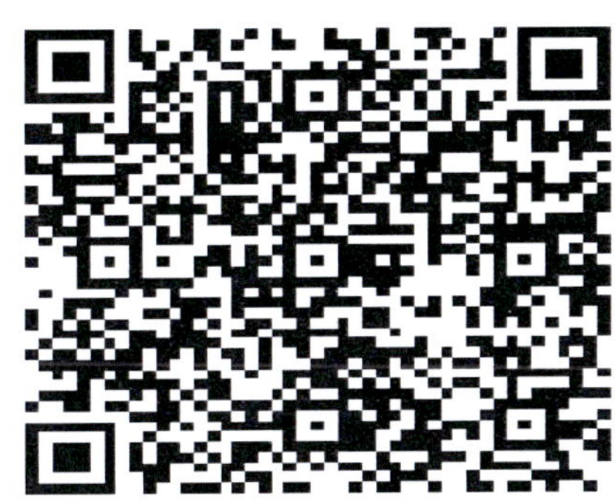

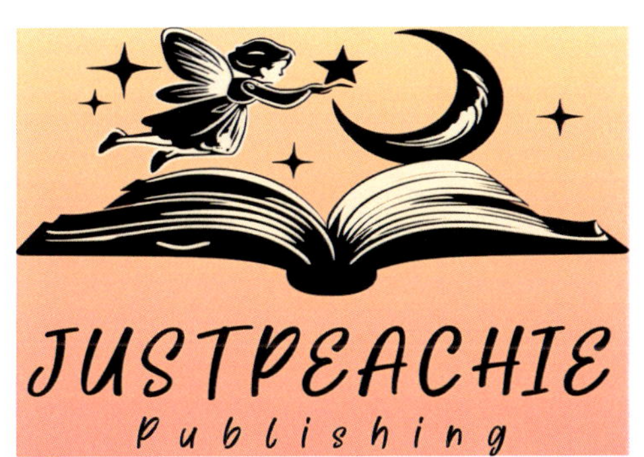

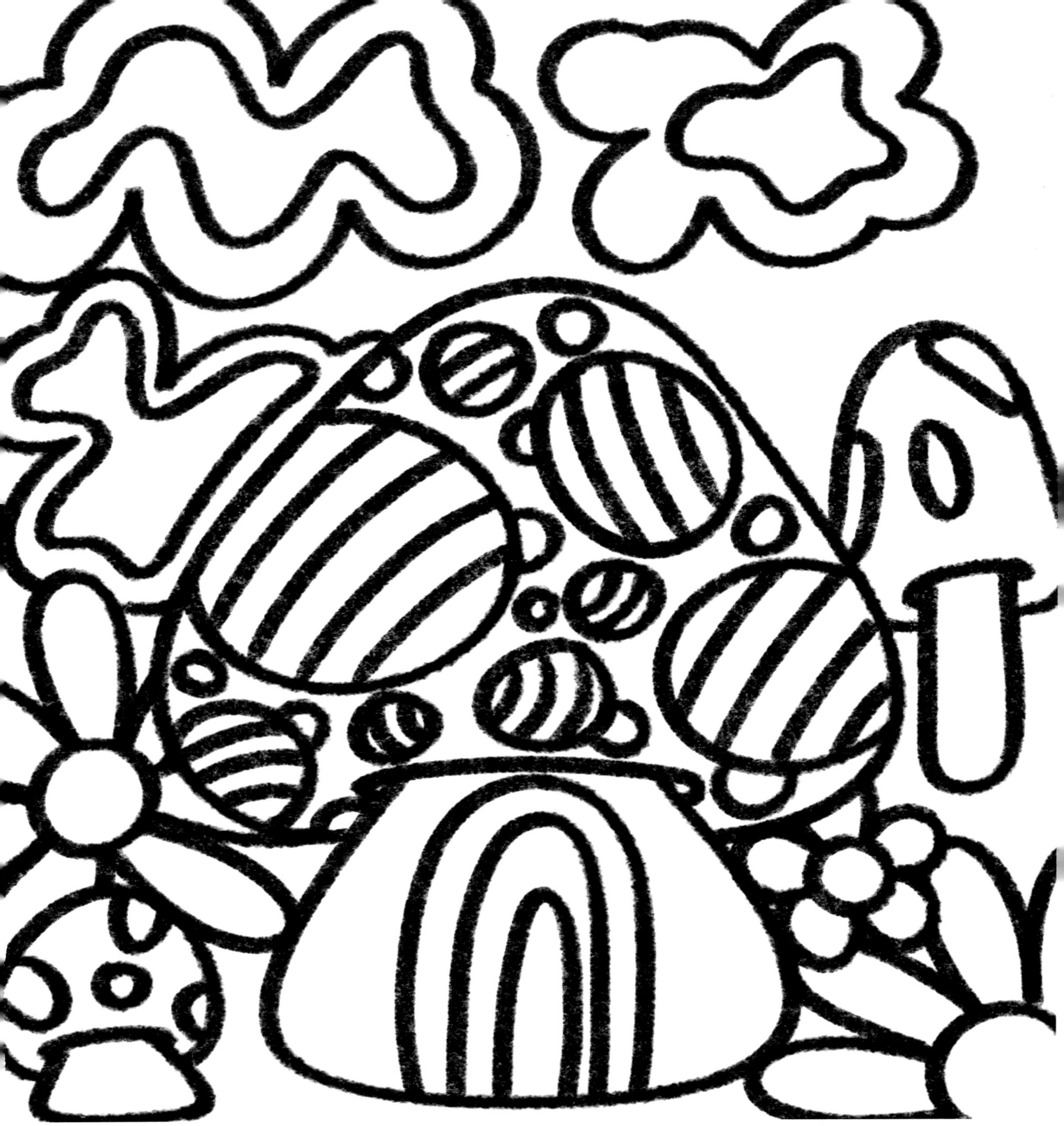

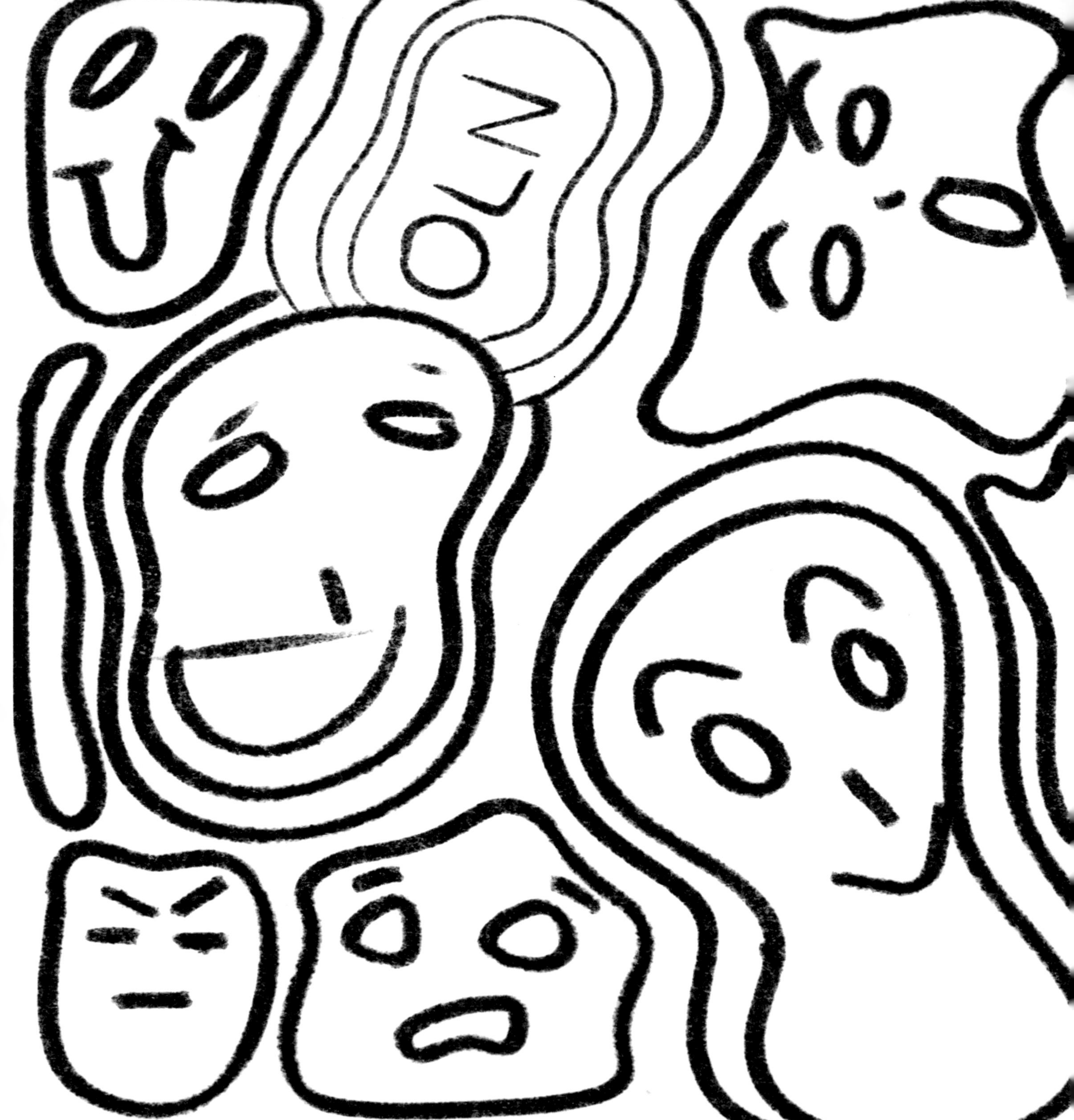

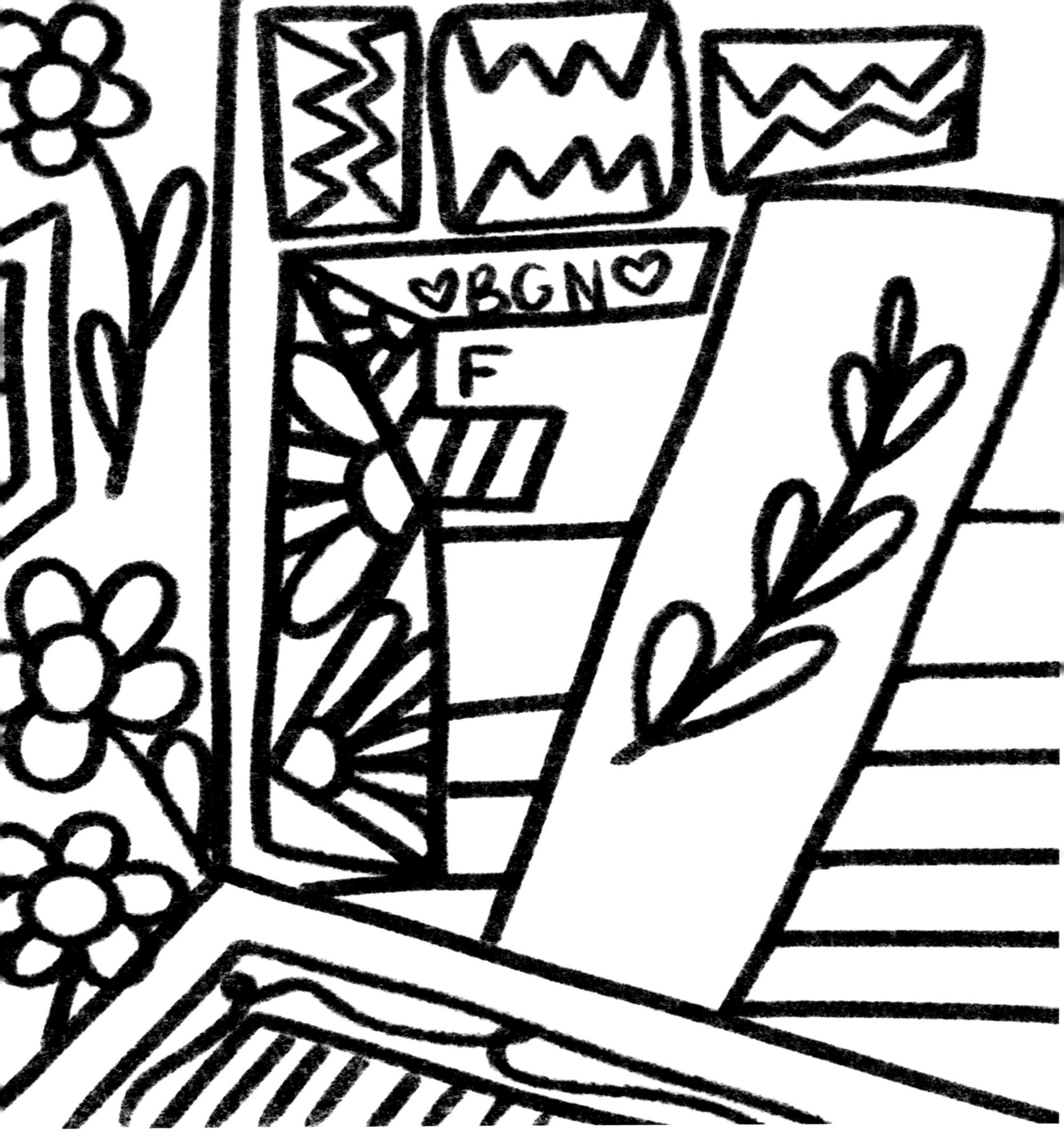

♥ B G N ♥
F

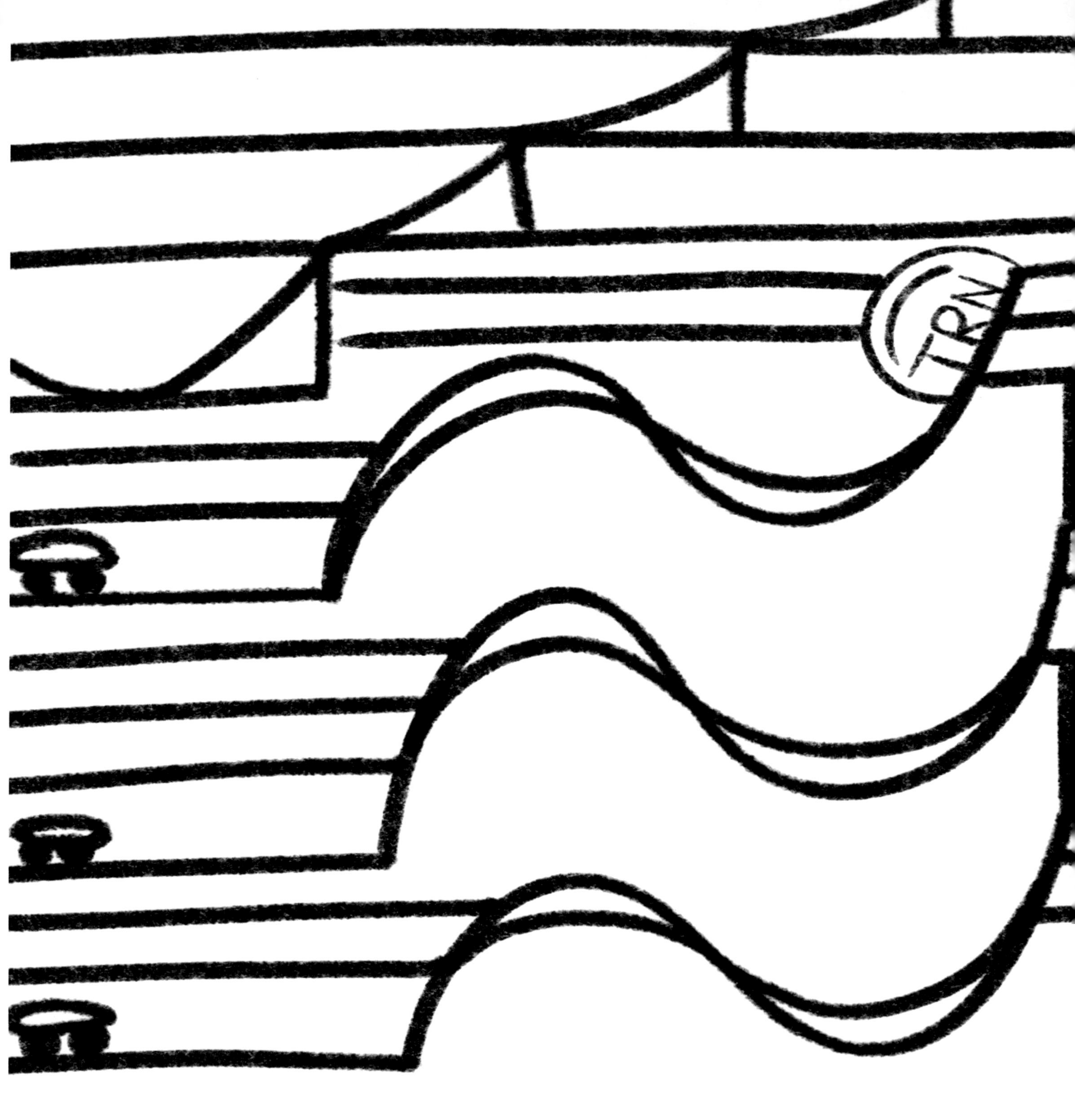
TRN

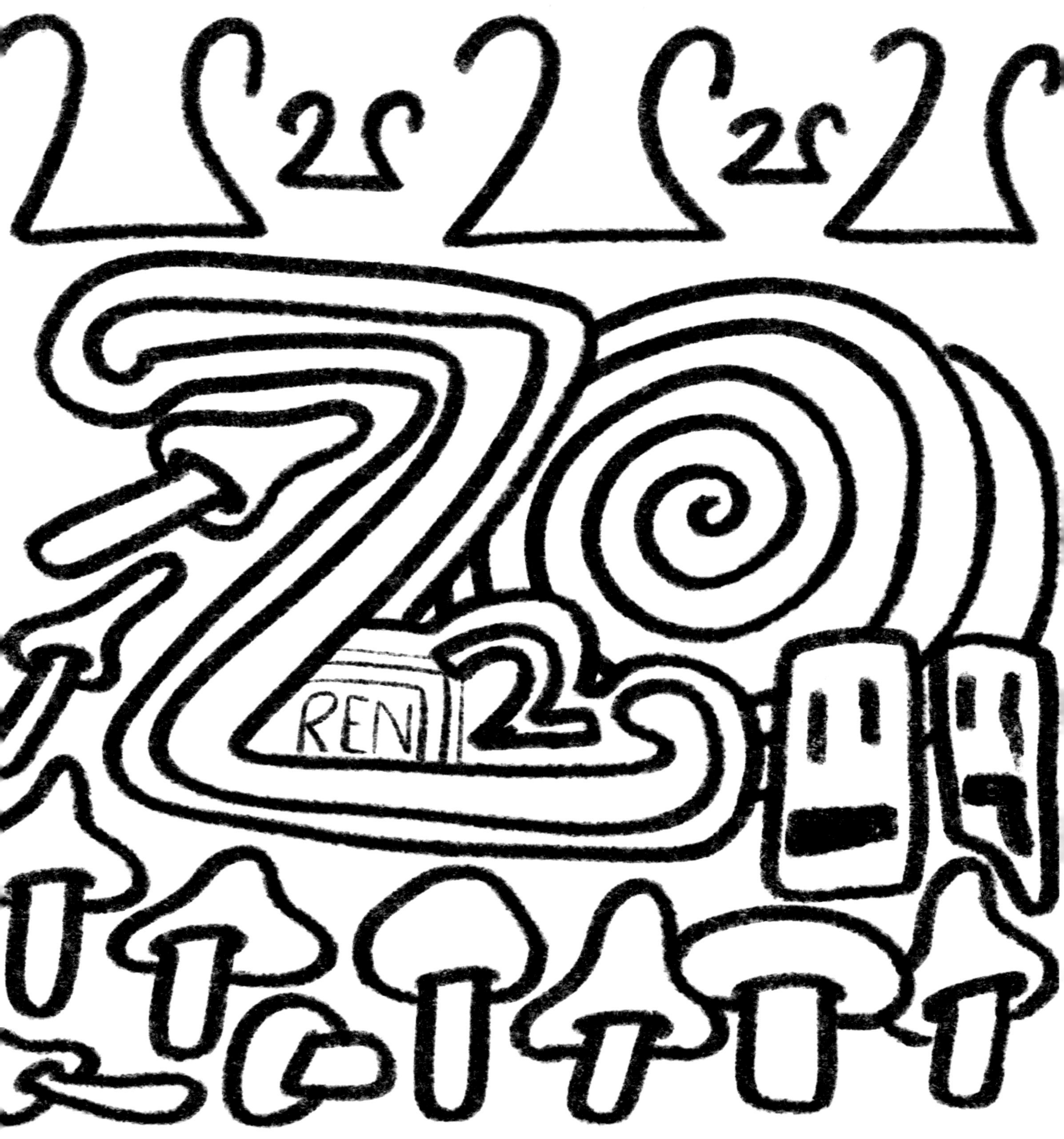
REN

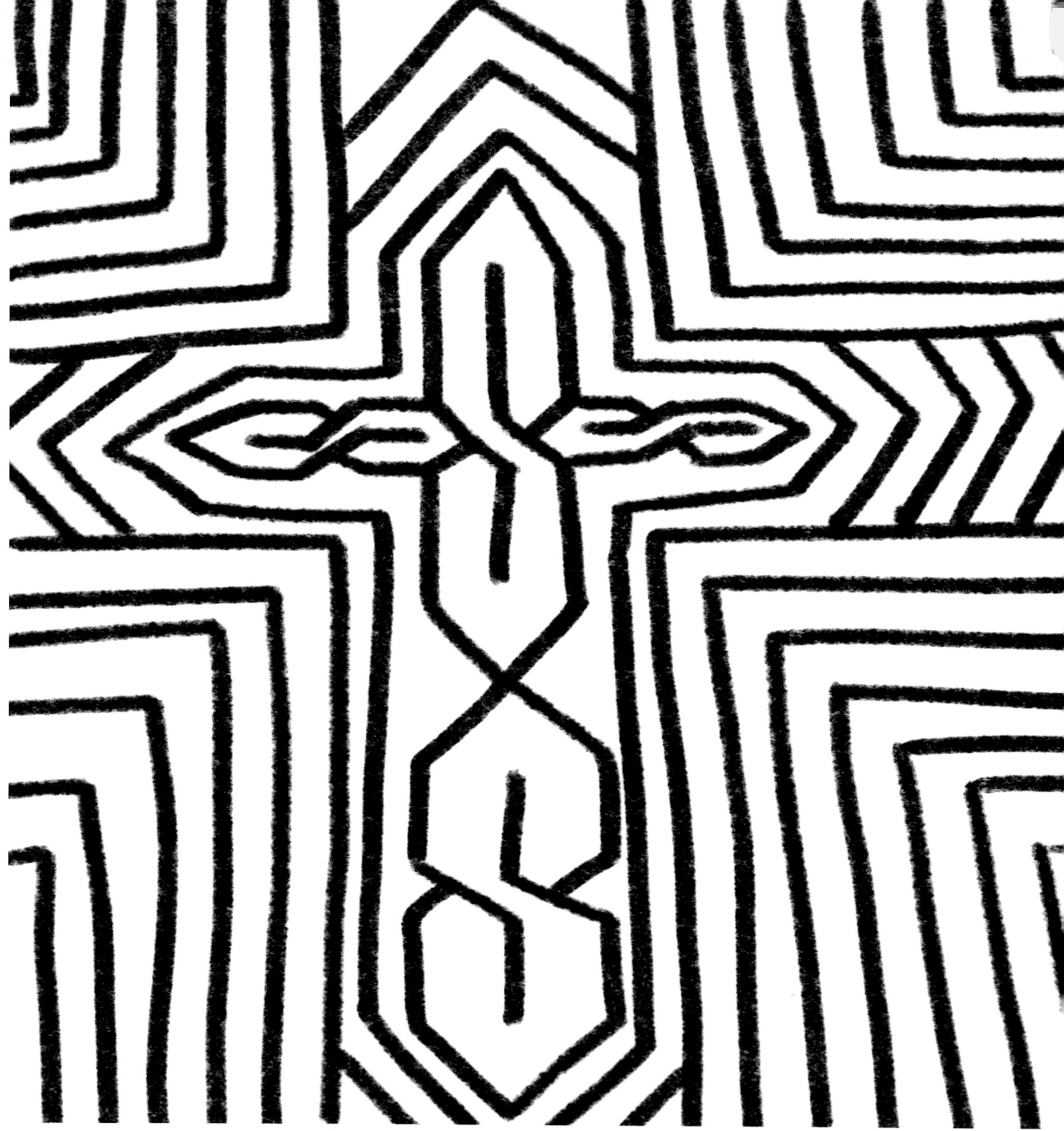

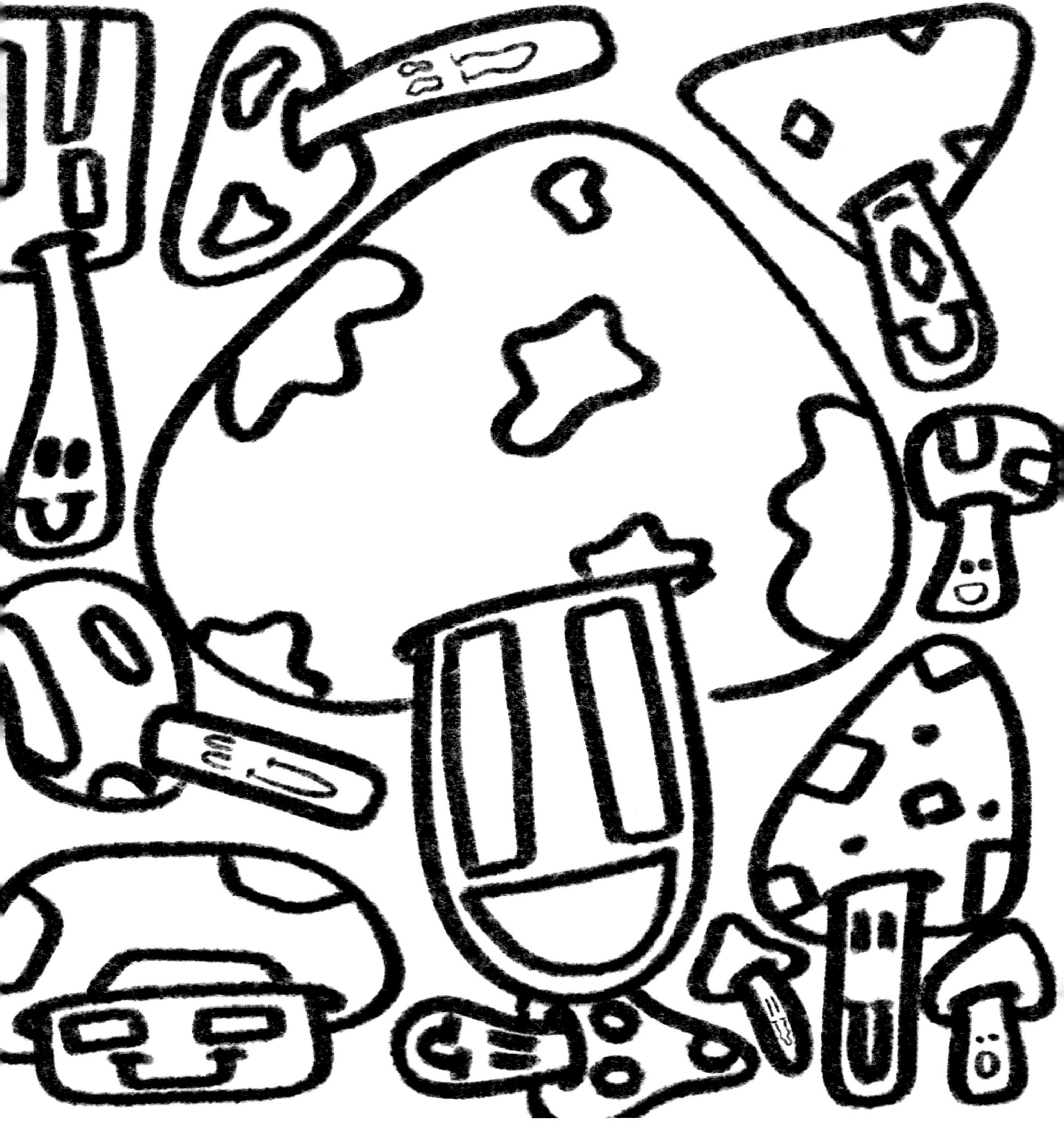

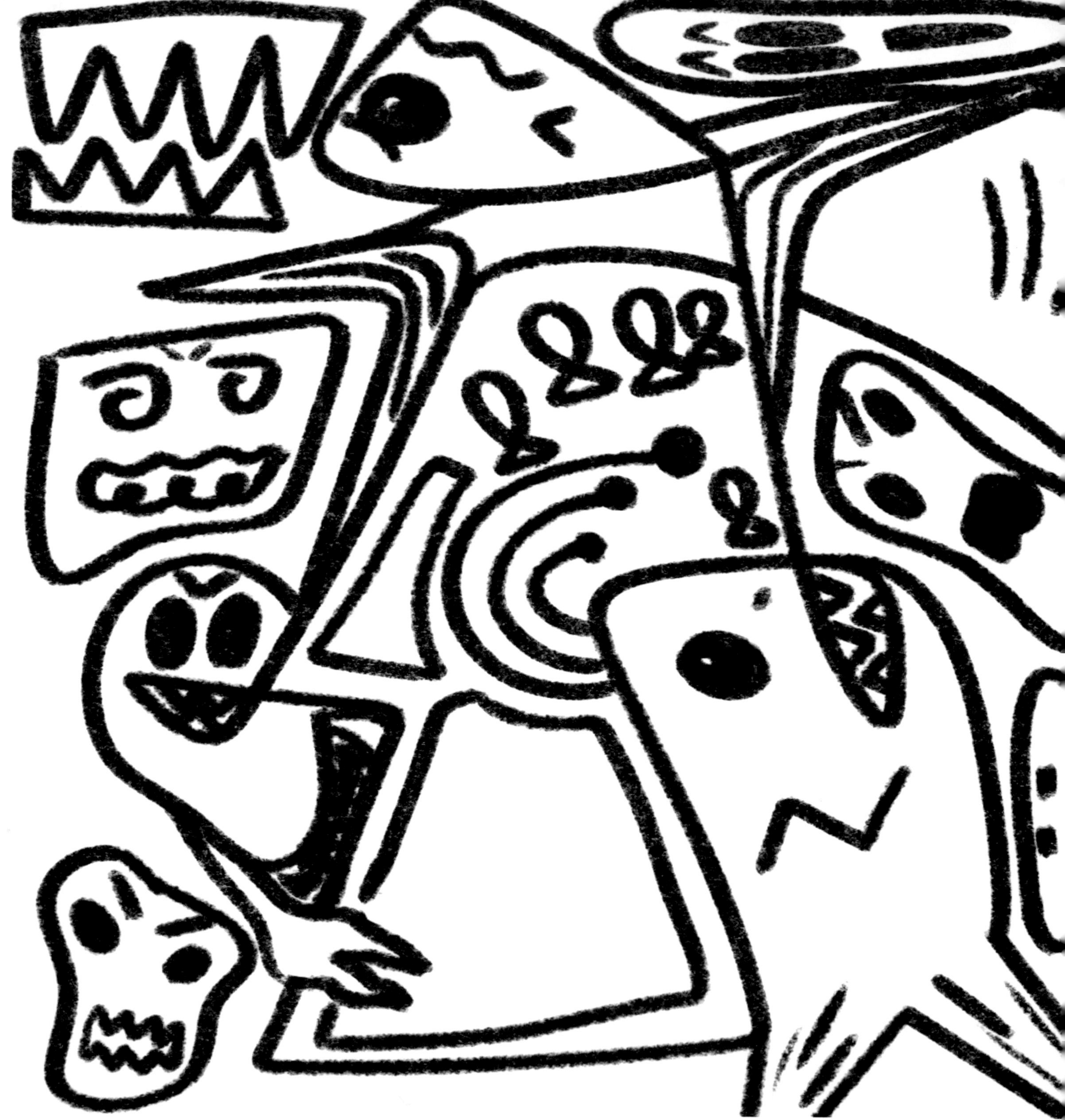

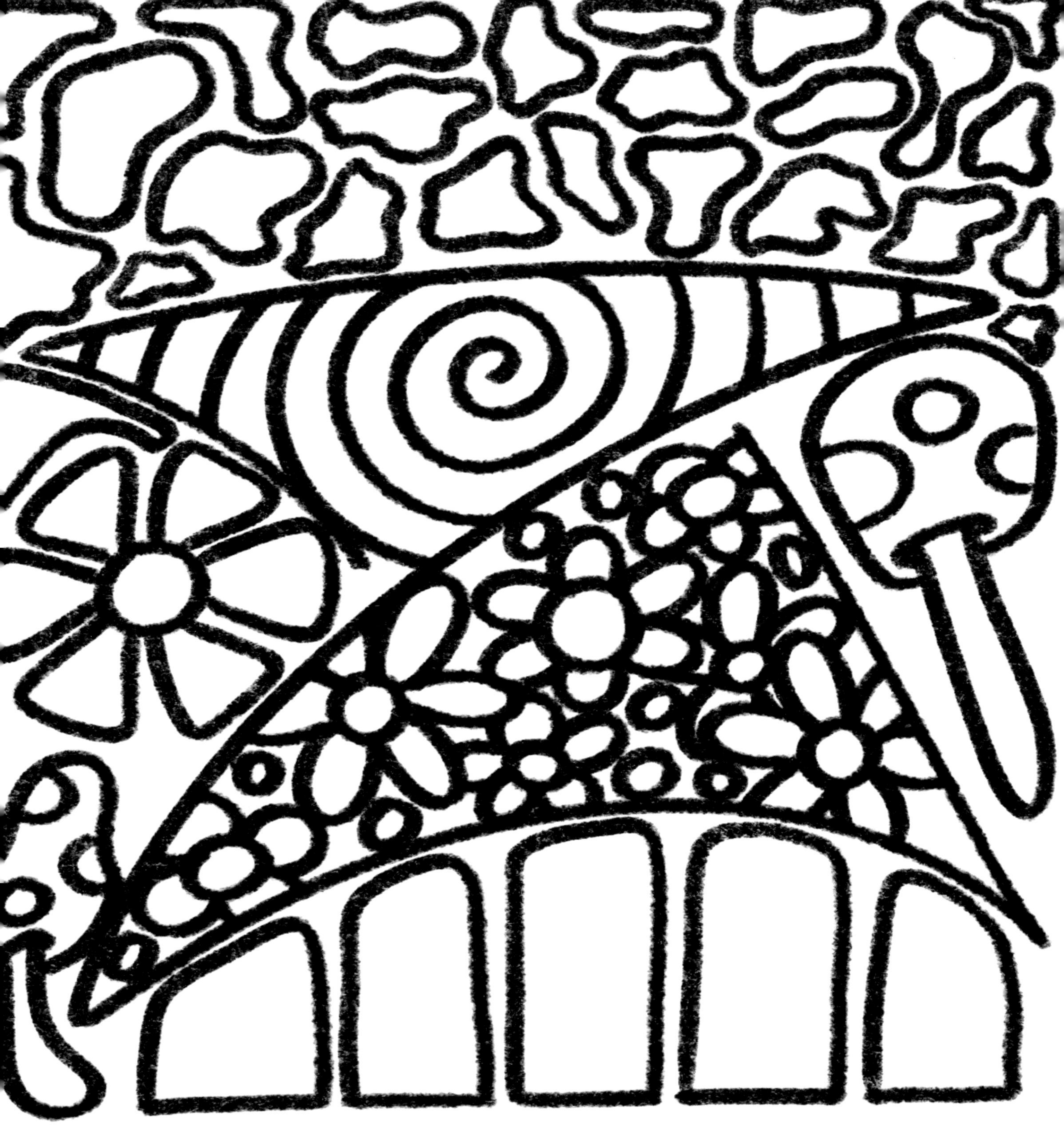

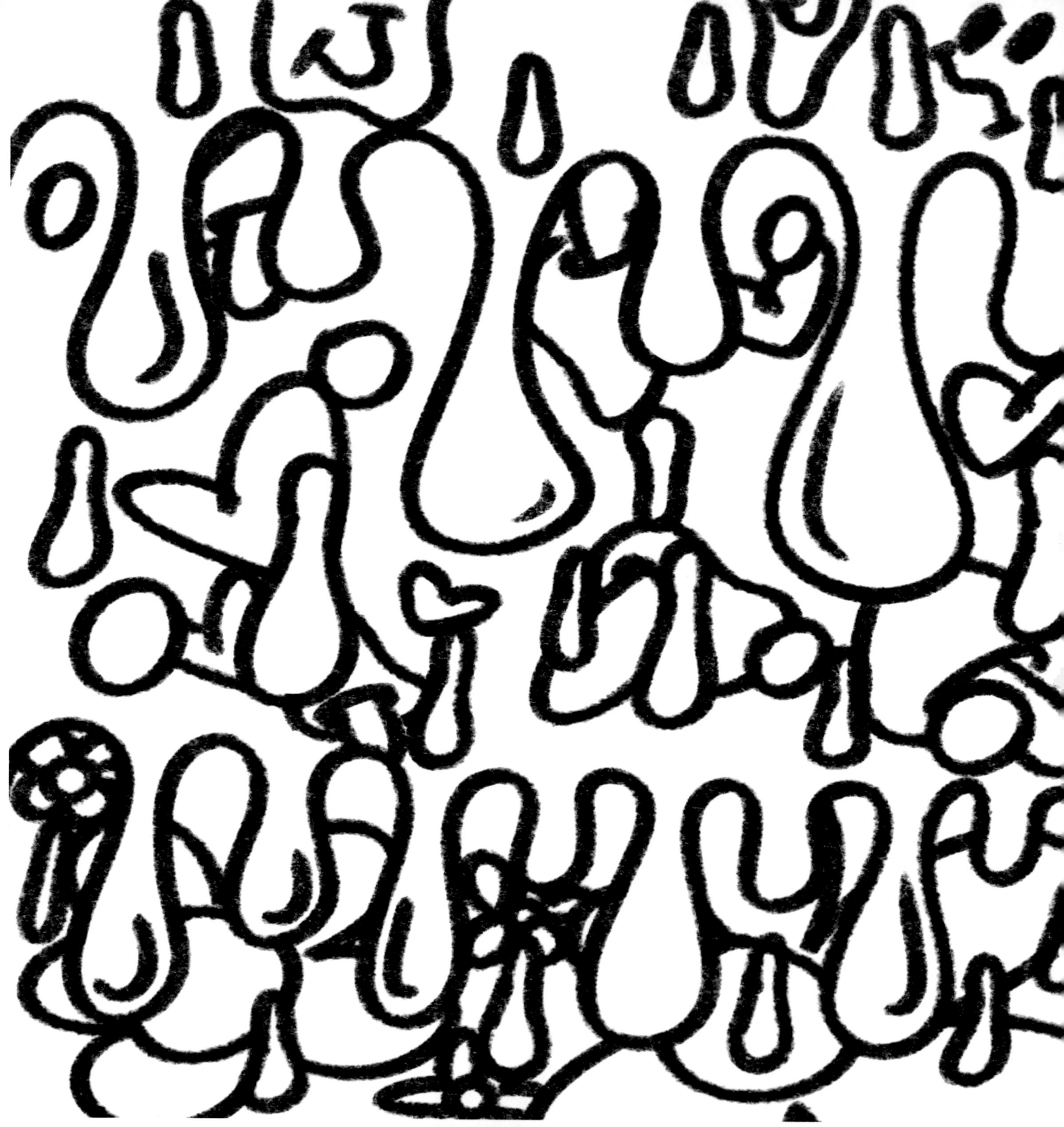

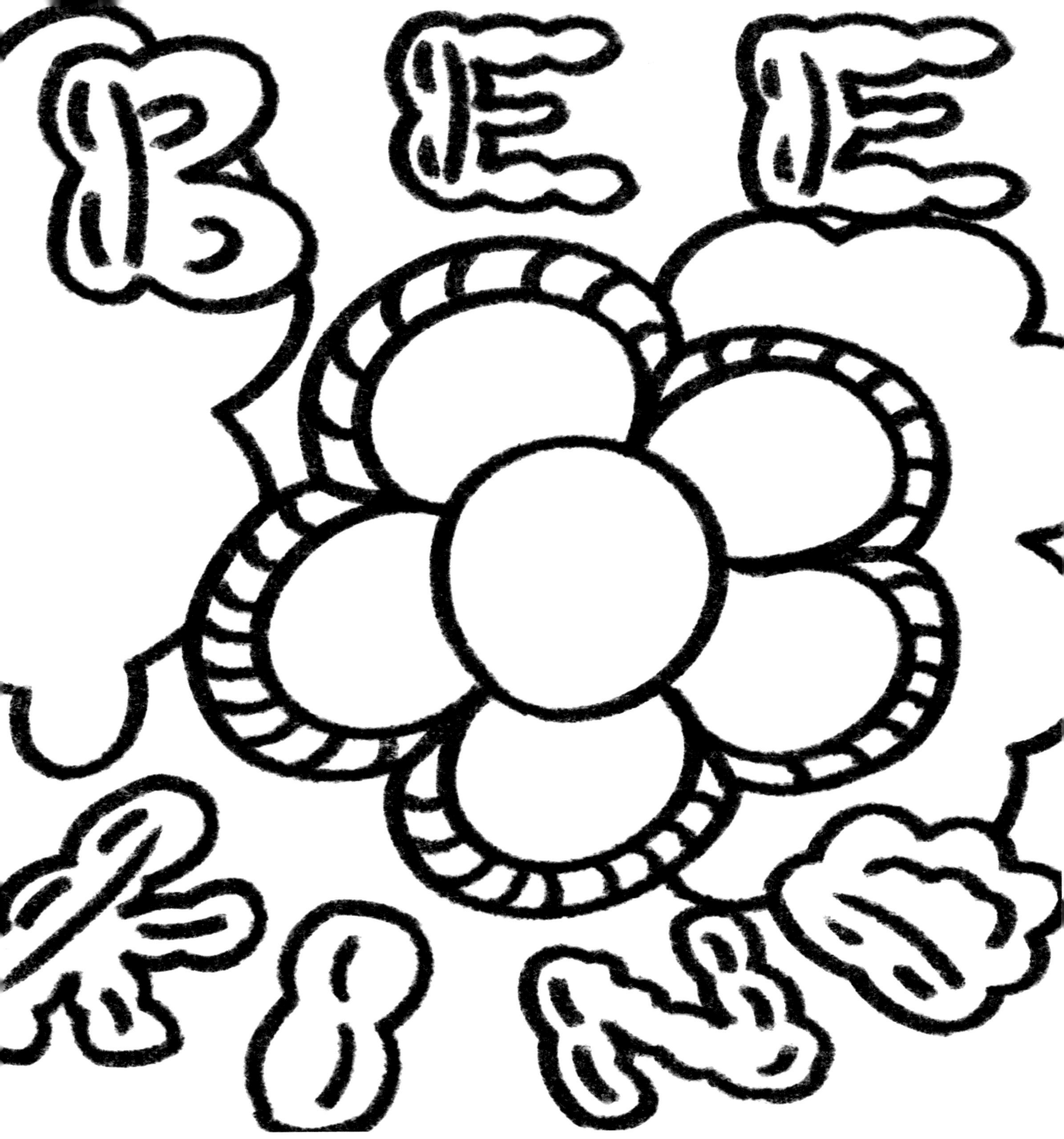

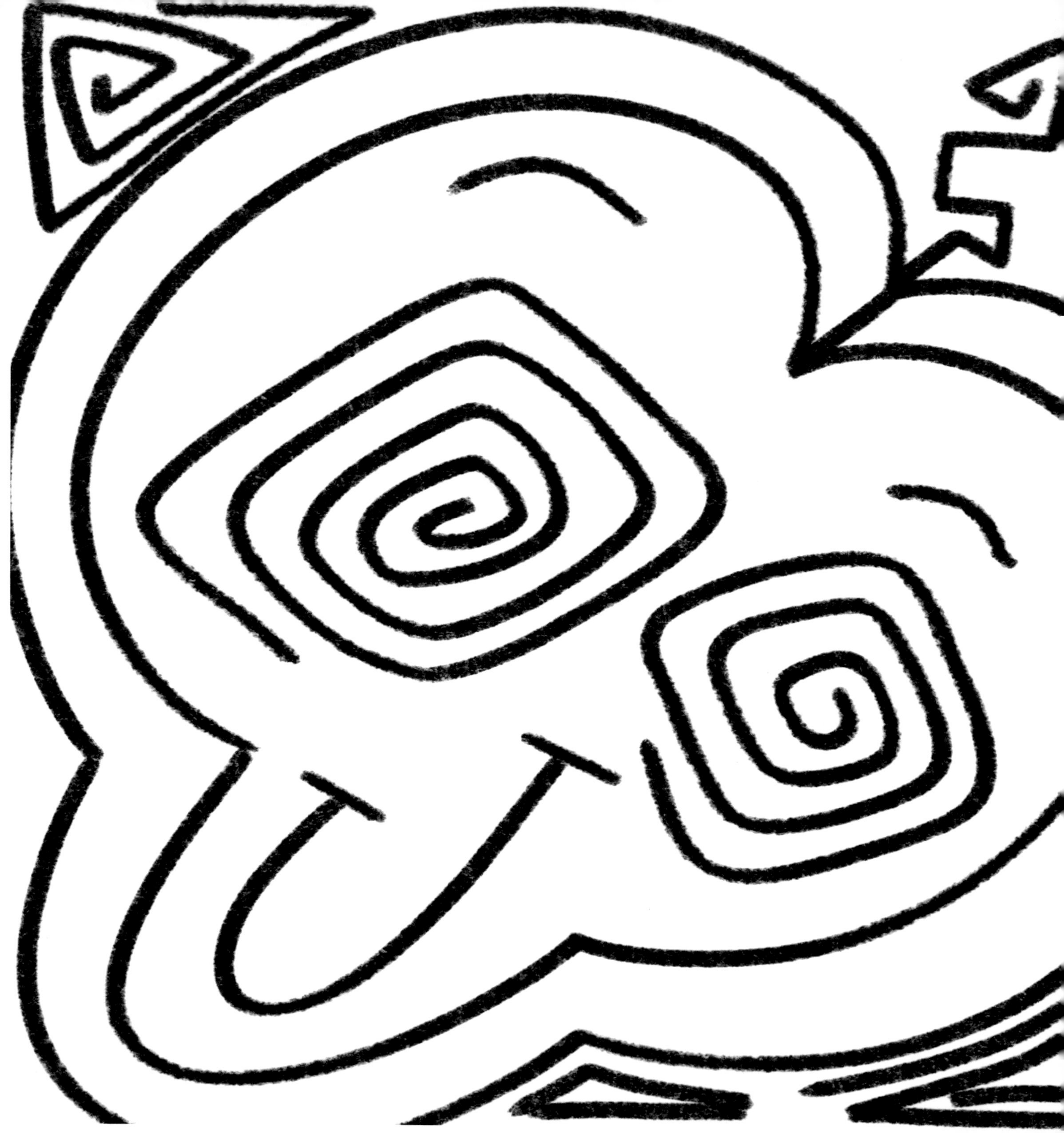

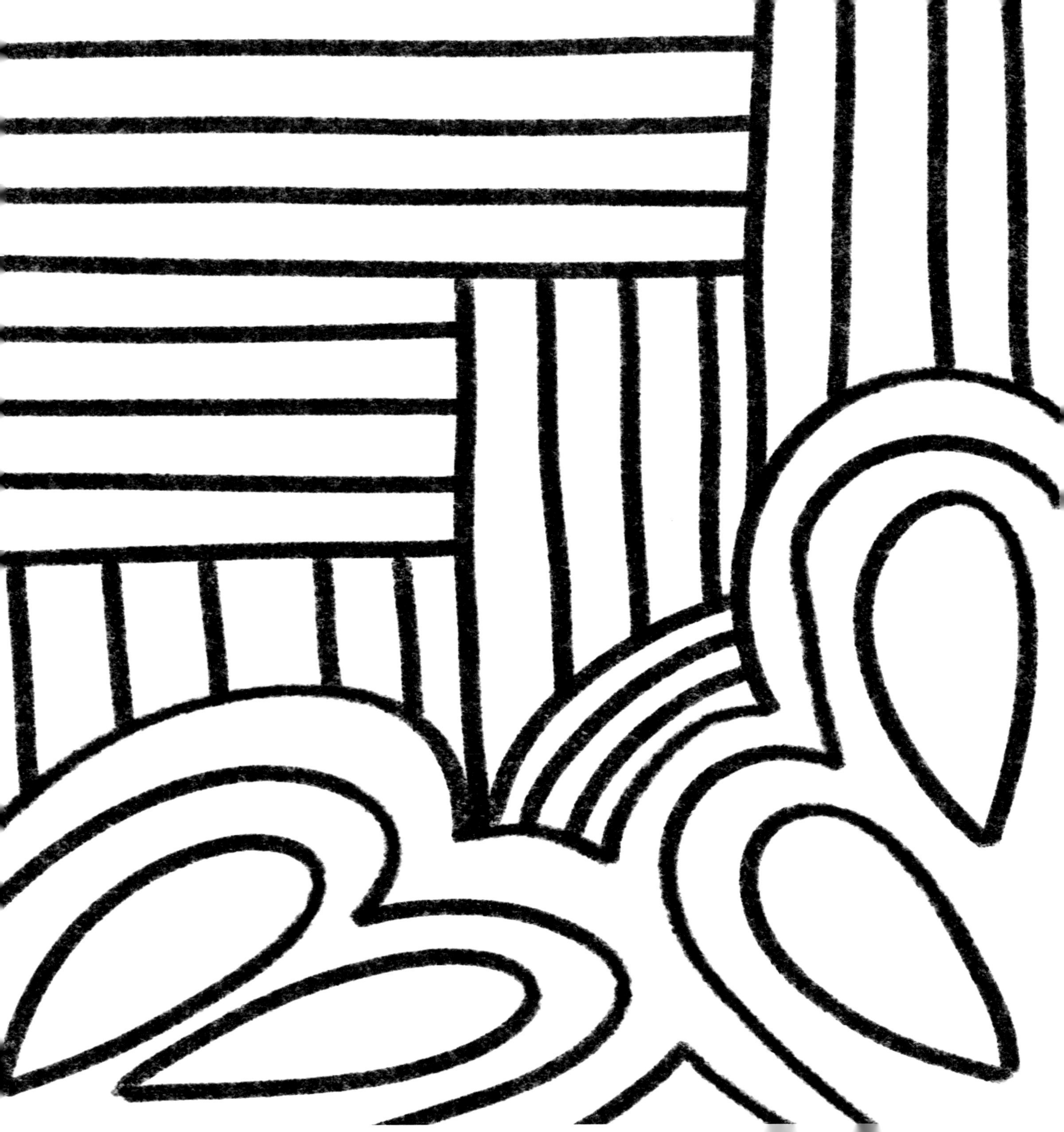

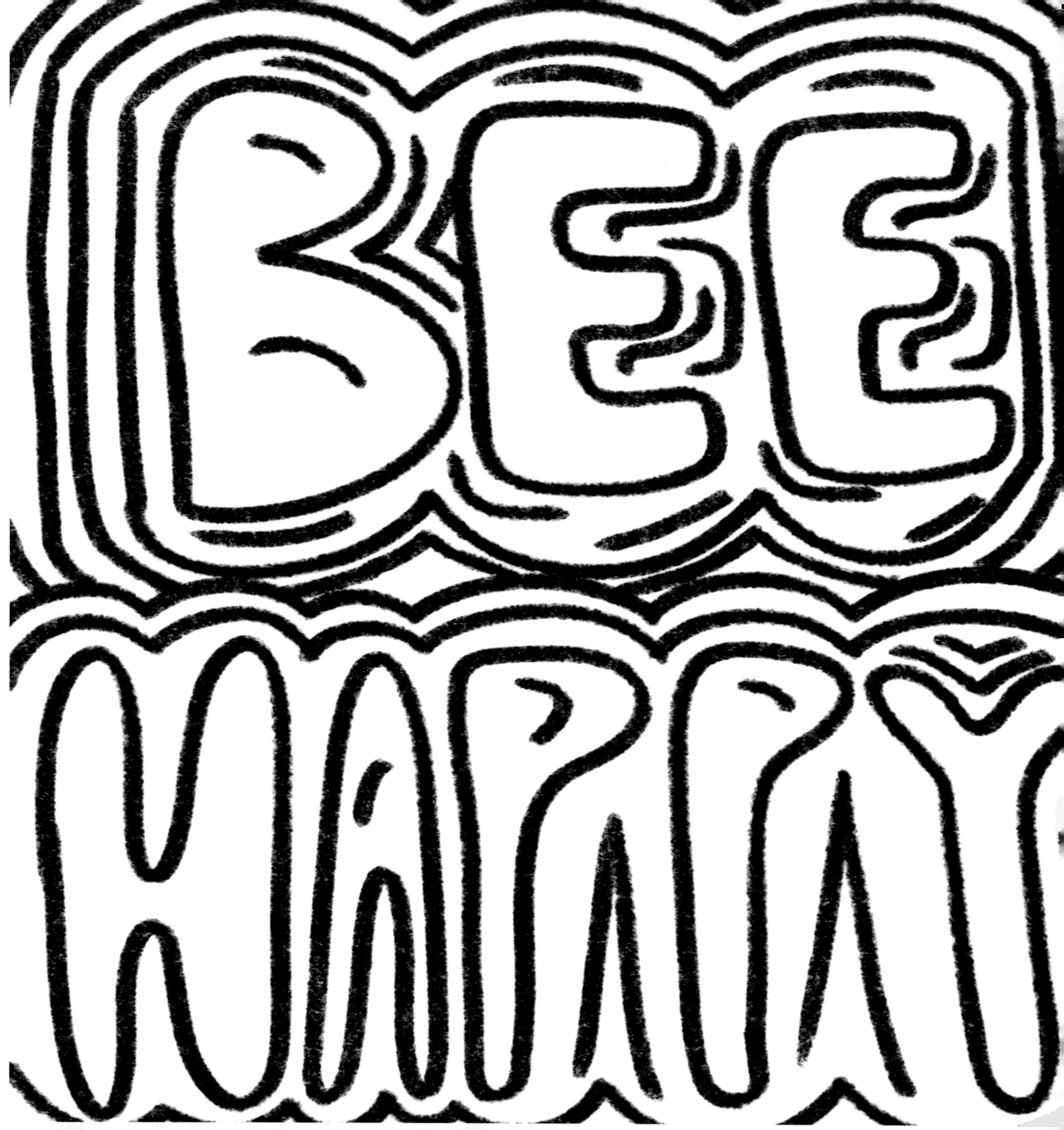

BEE
HAPPY

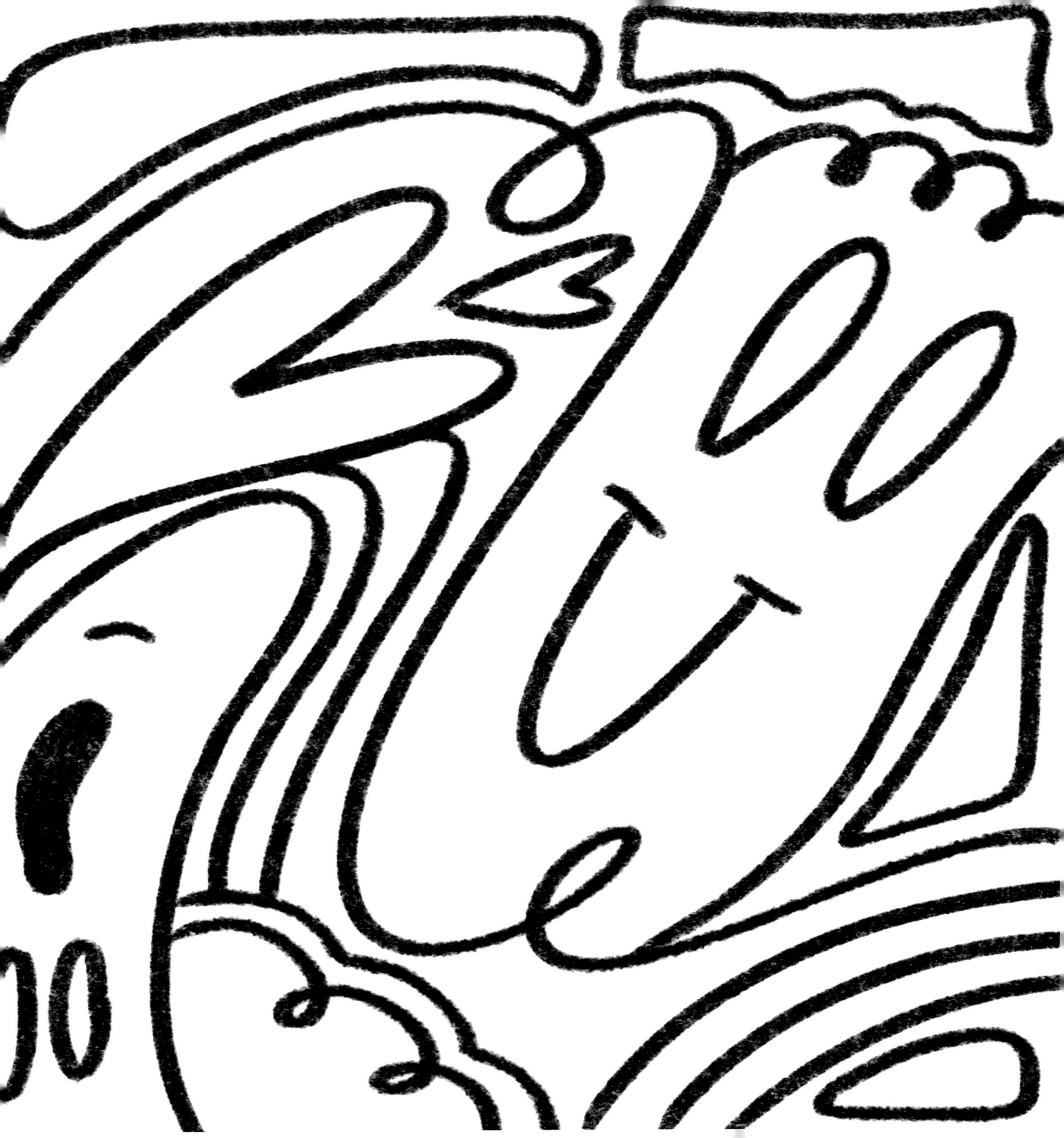

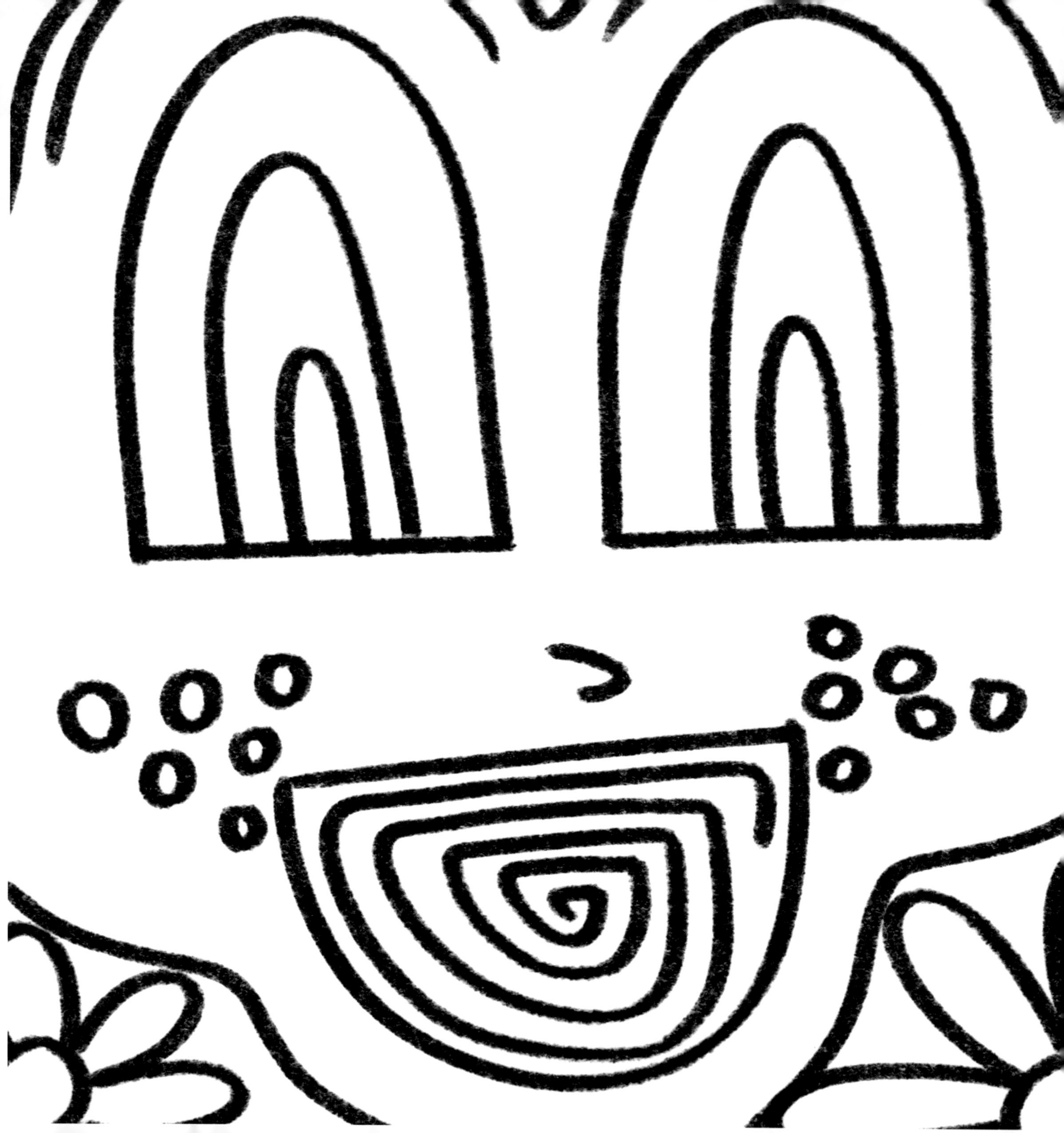

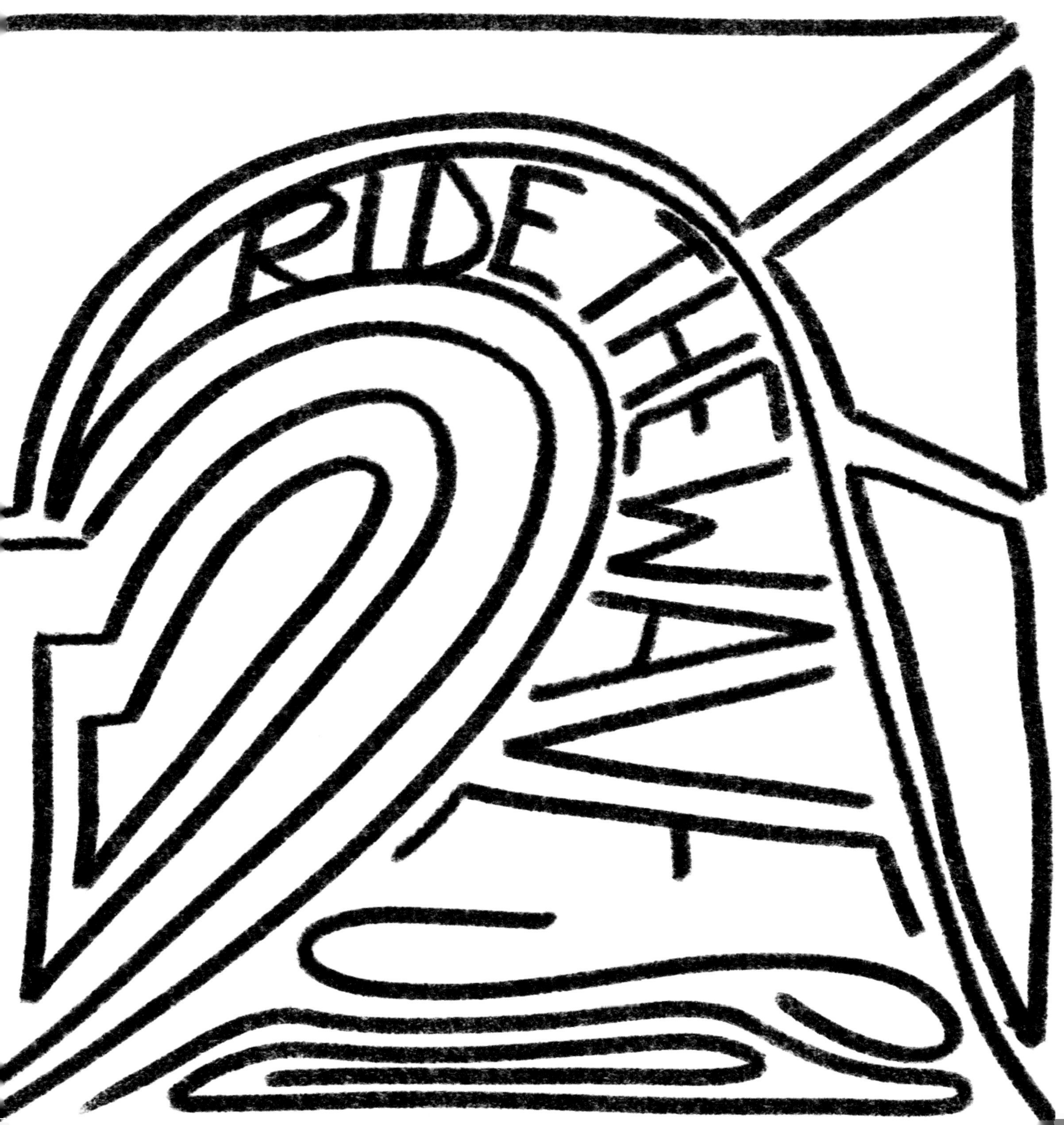

RIDE THE WAVE
2

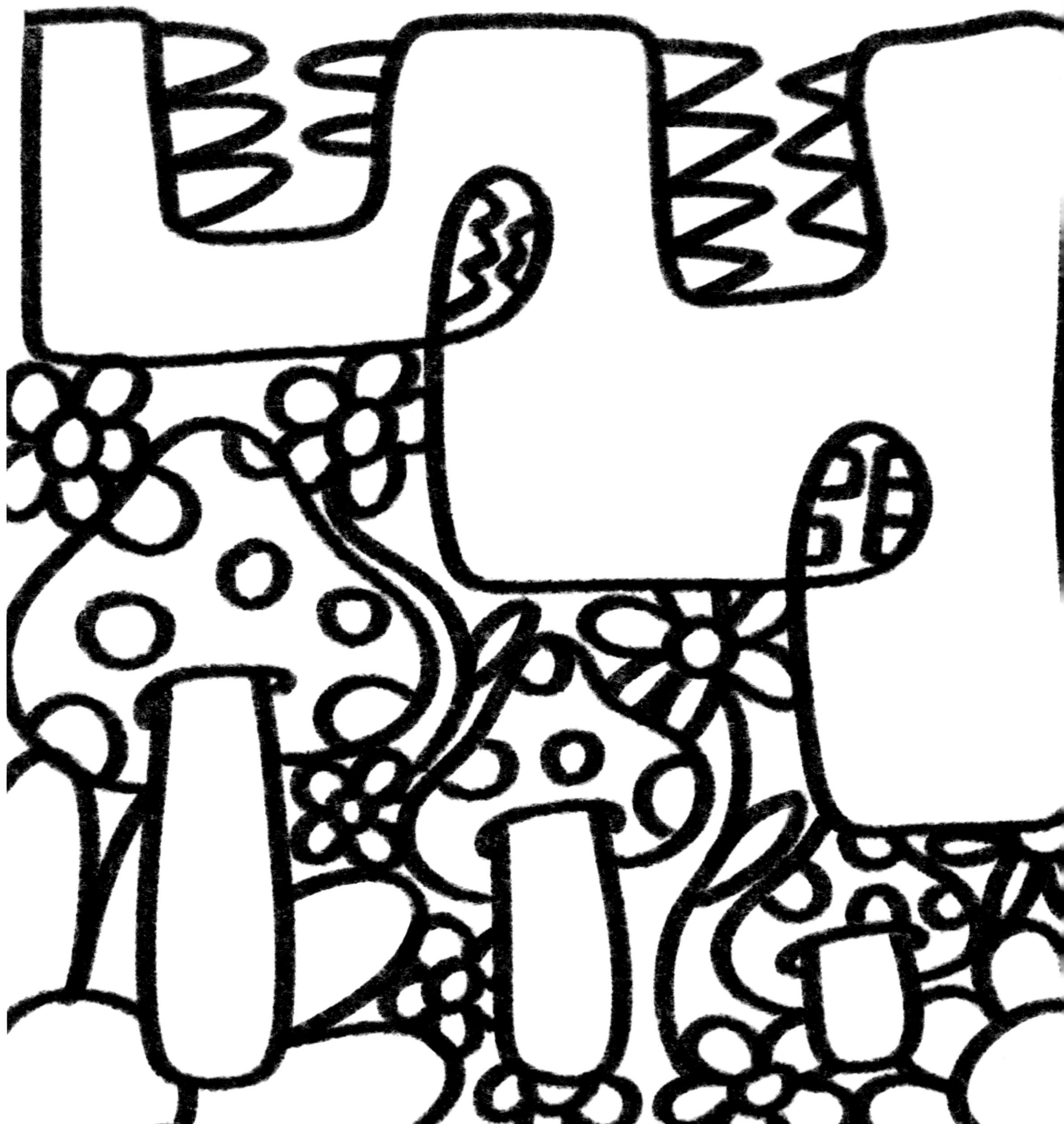

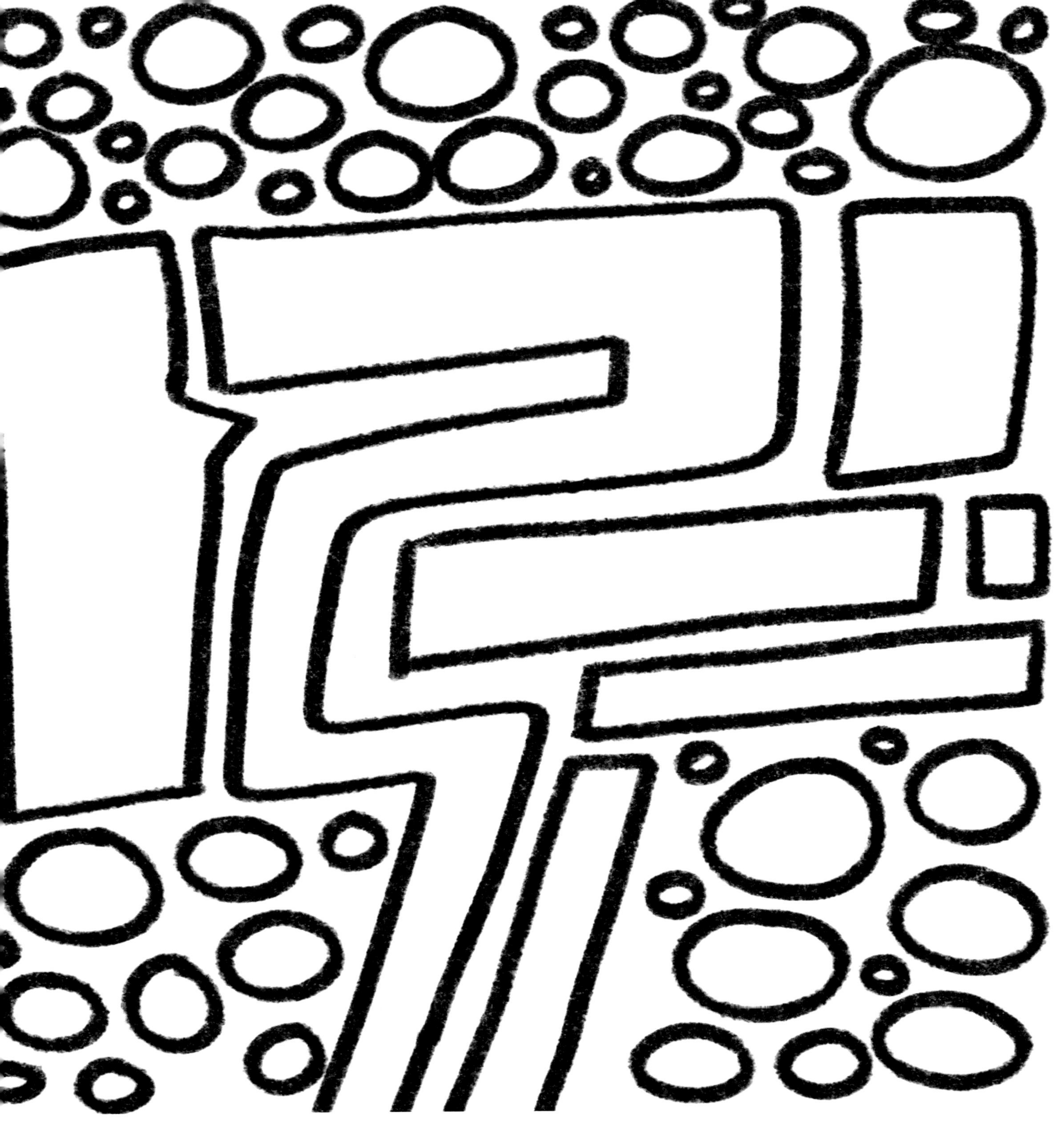

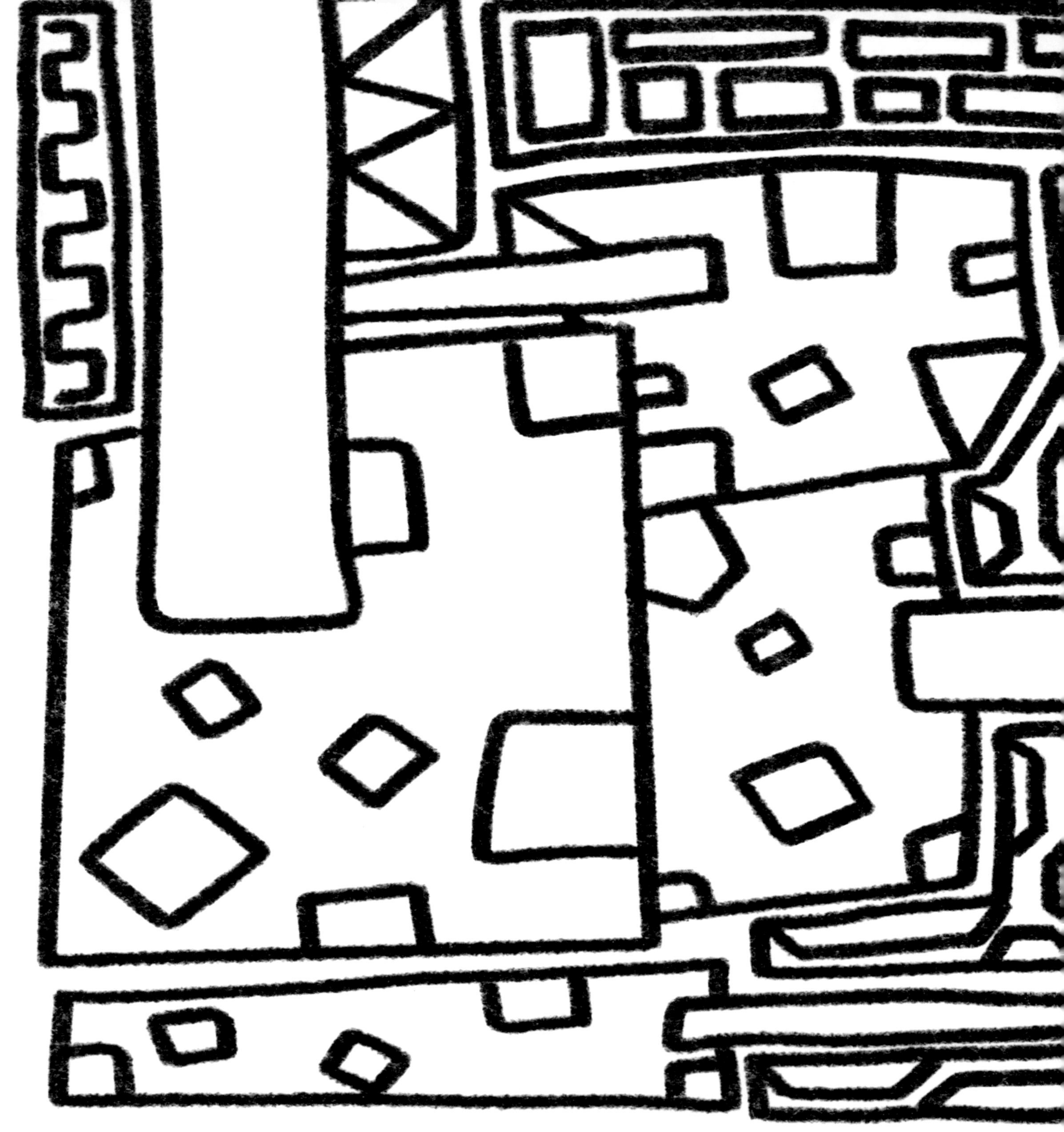

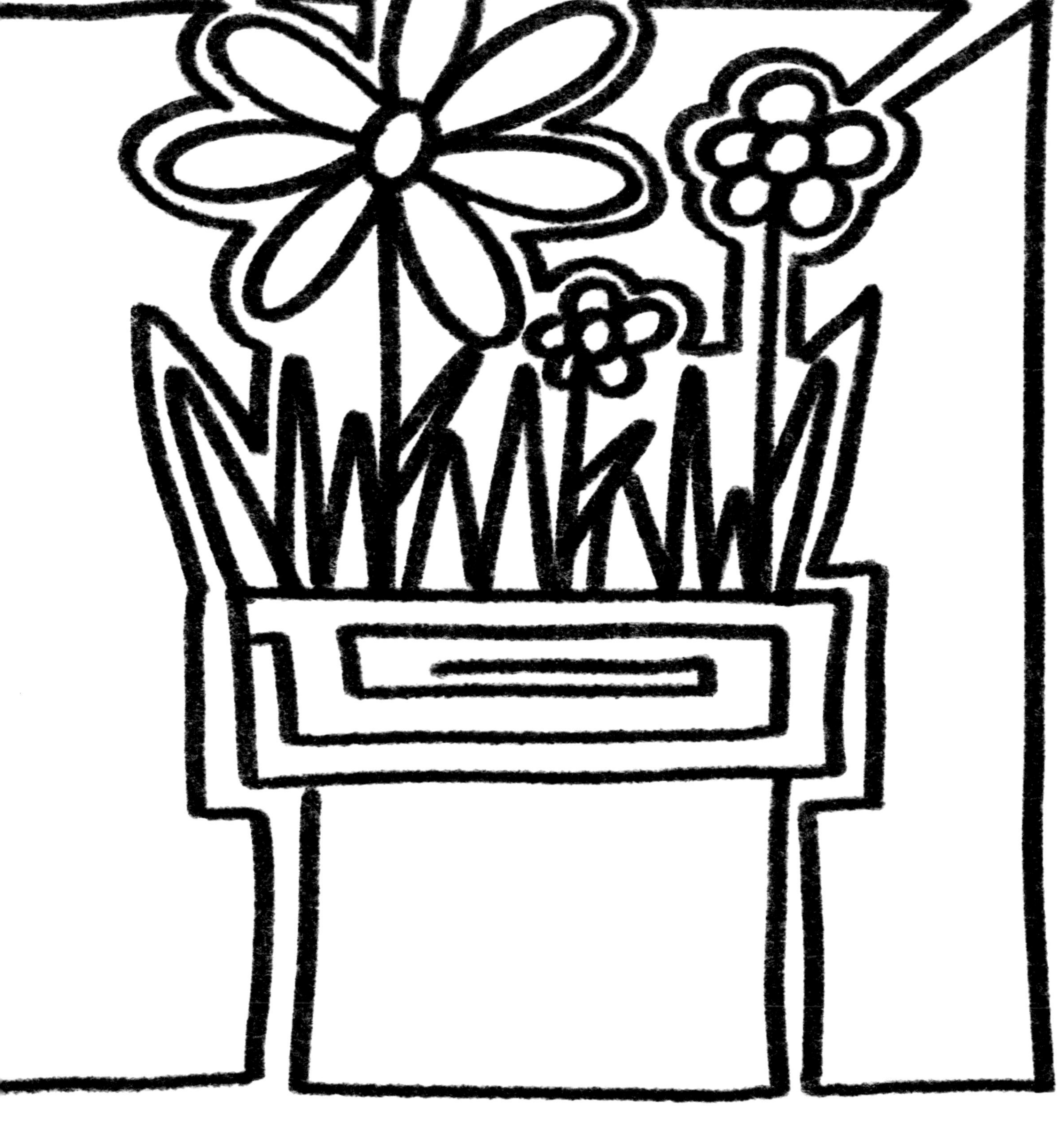

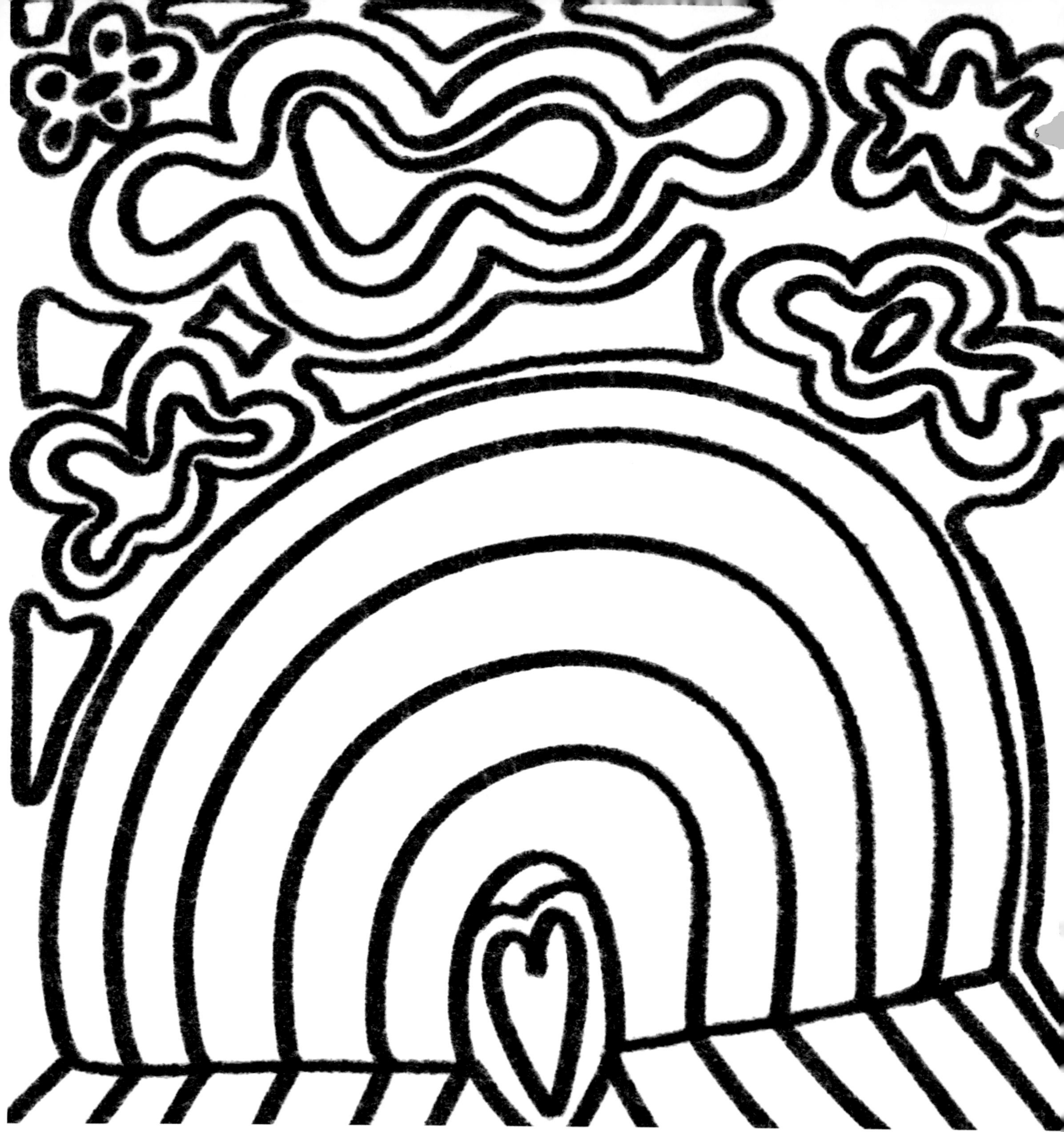

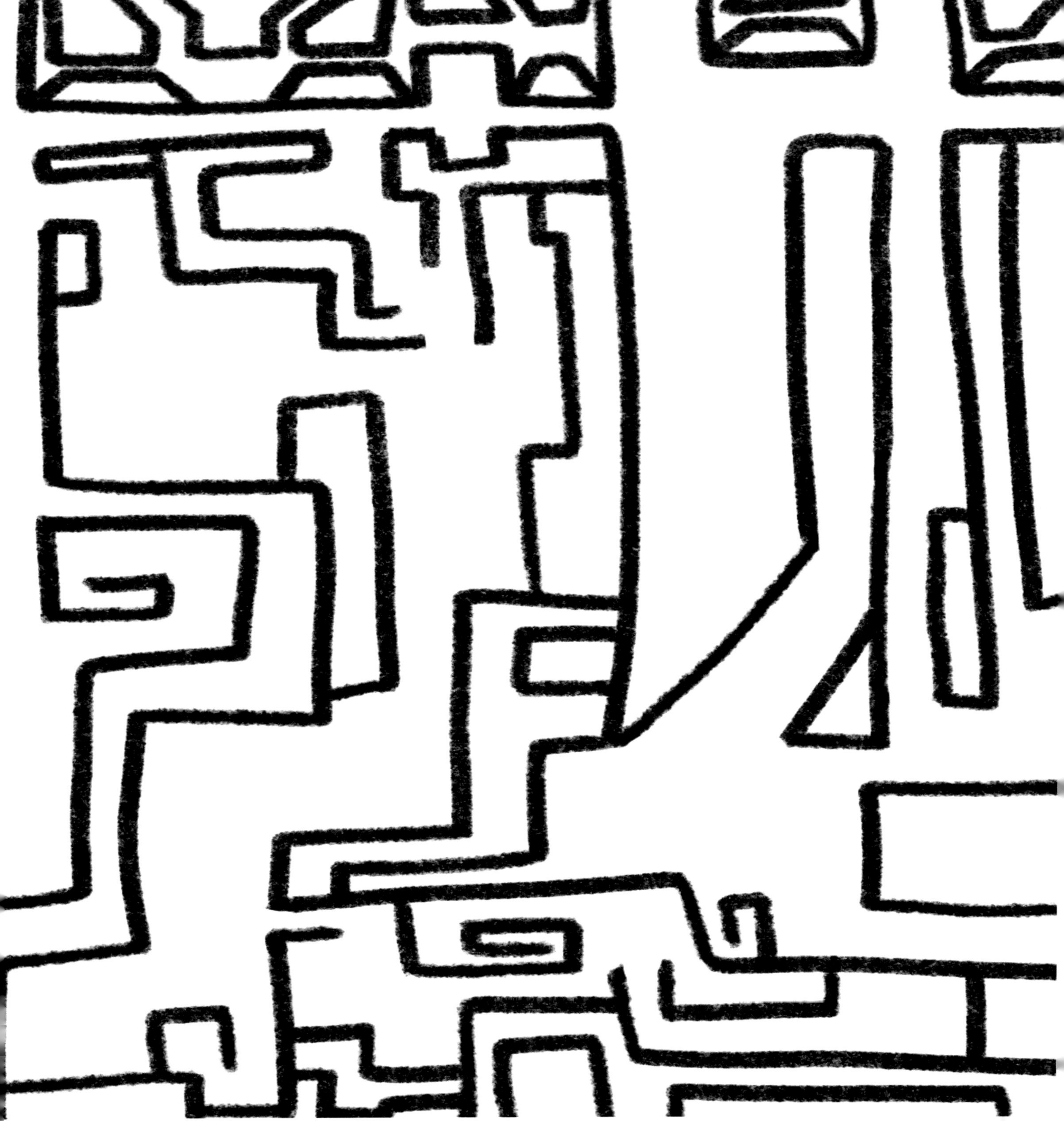

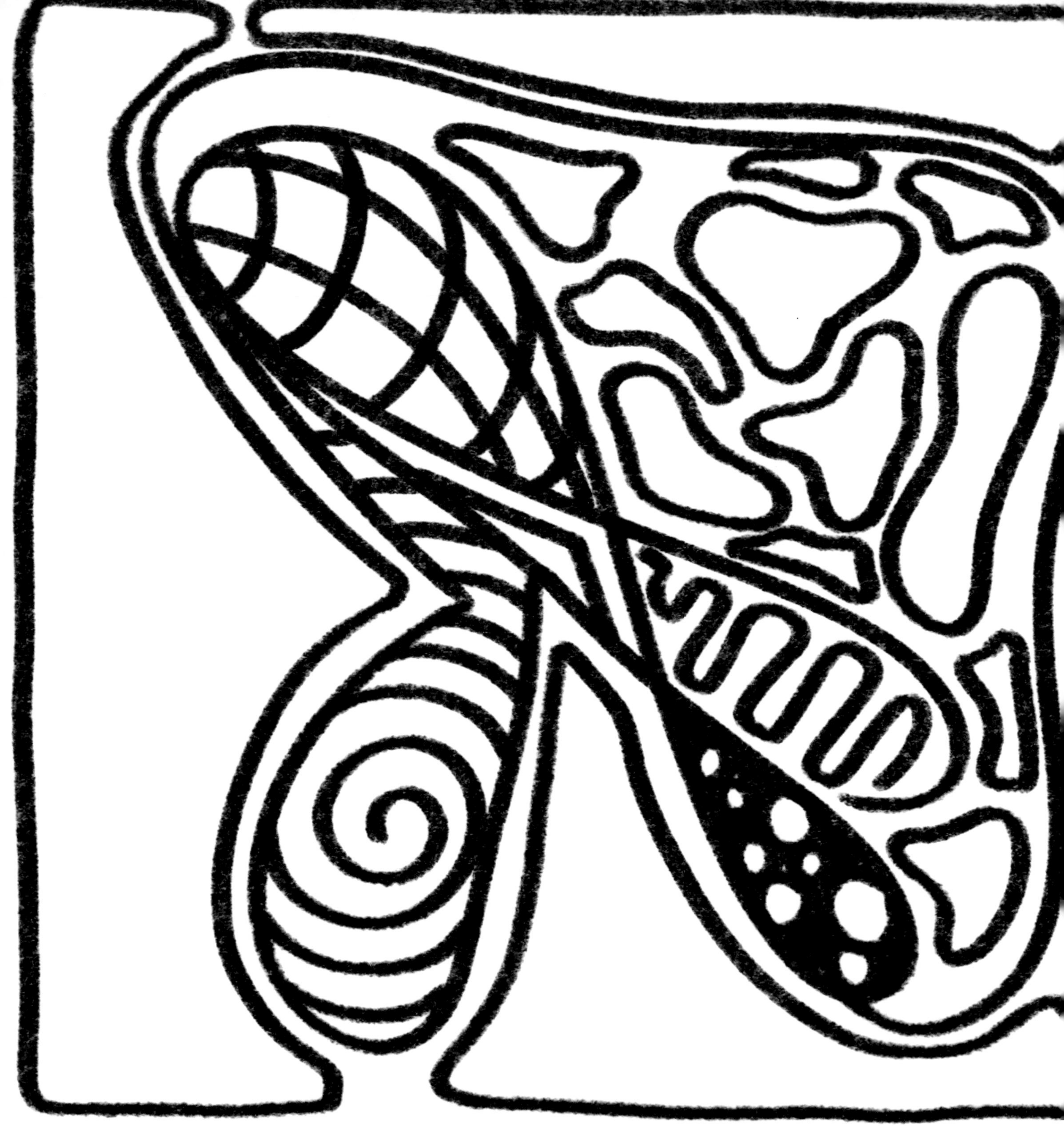

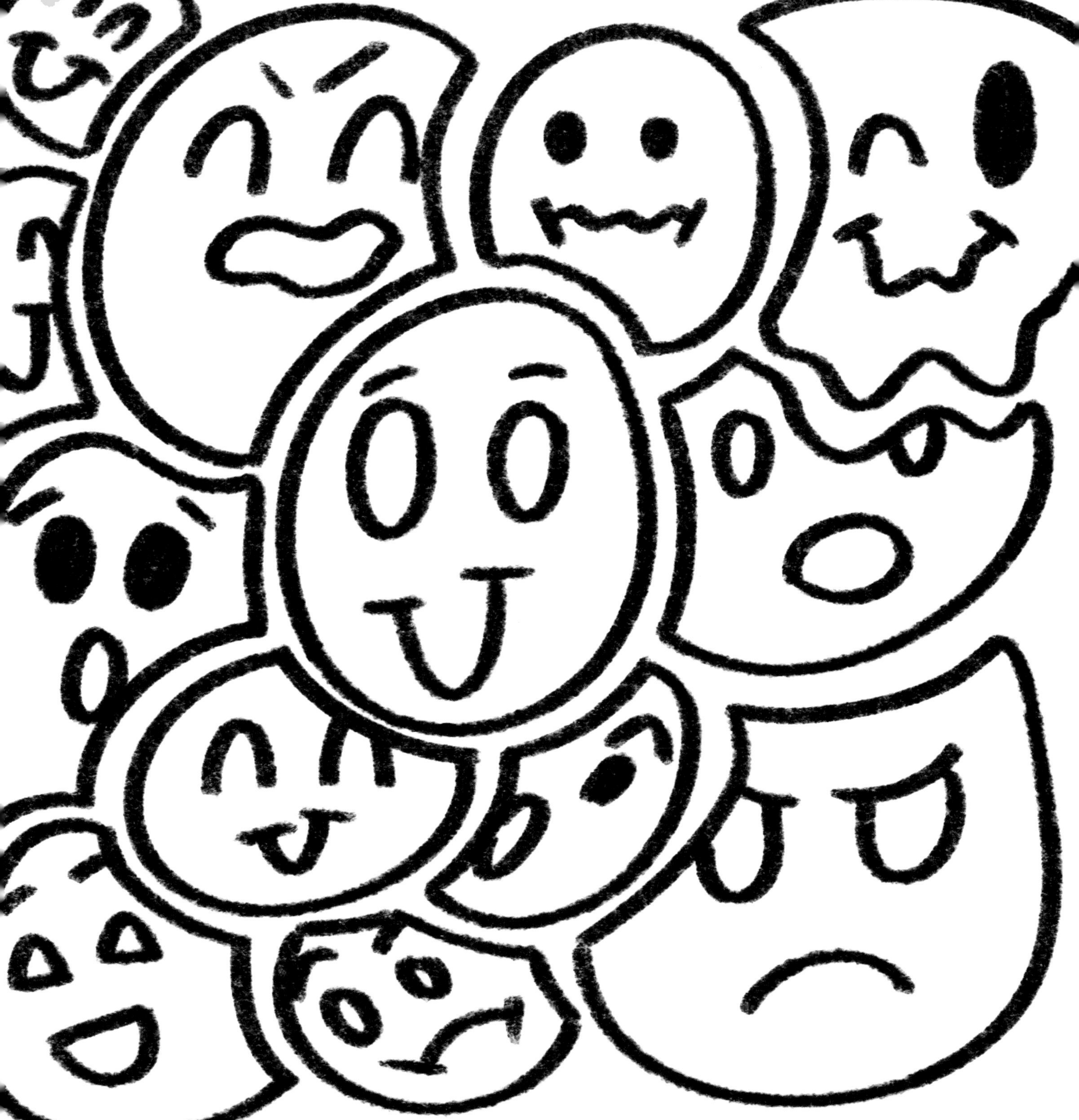

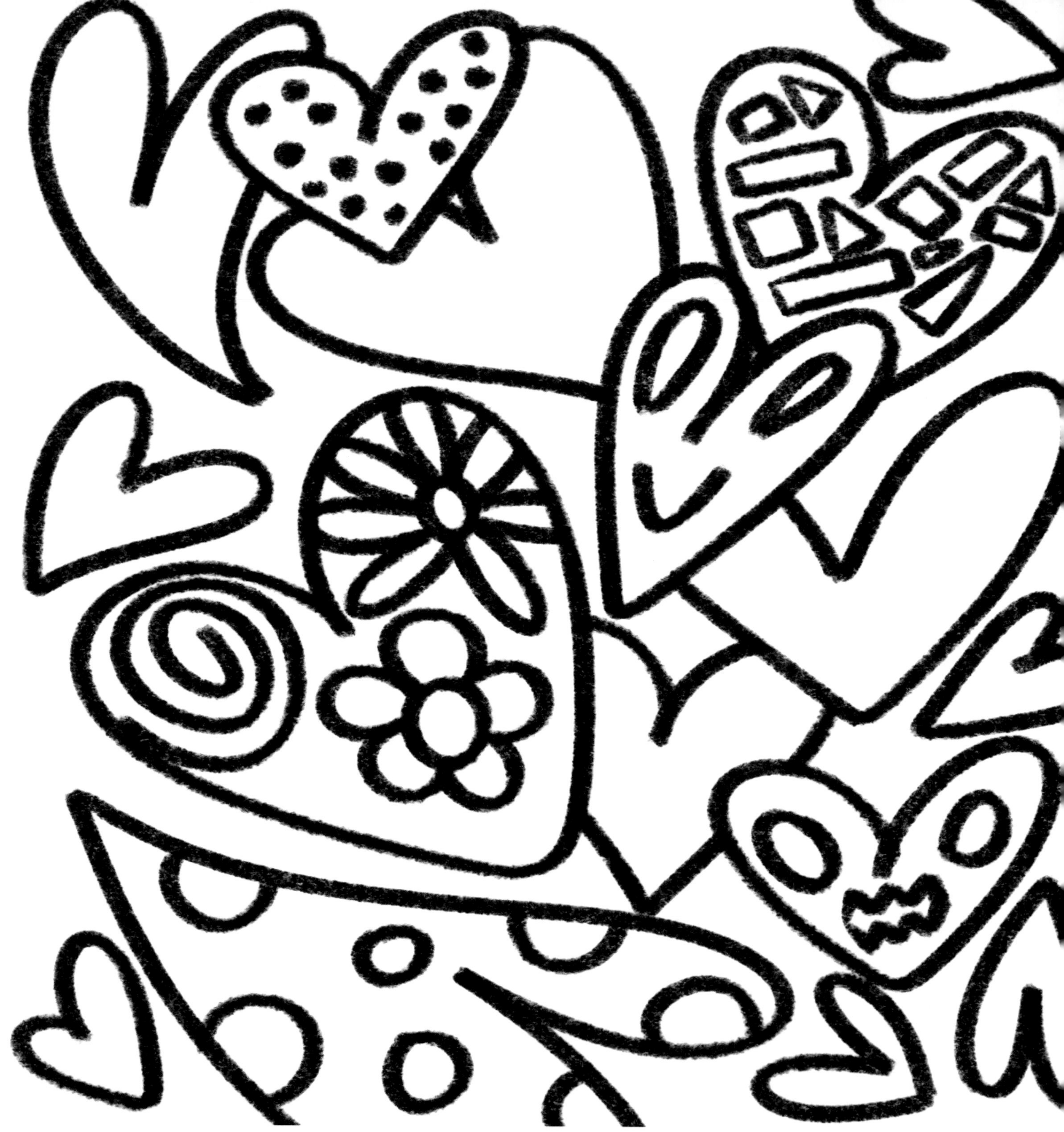

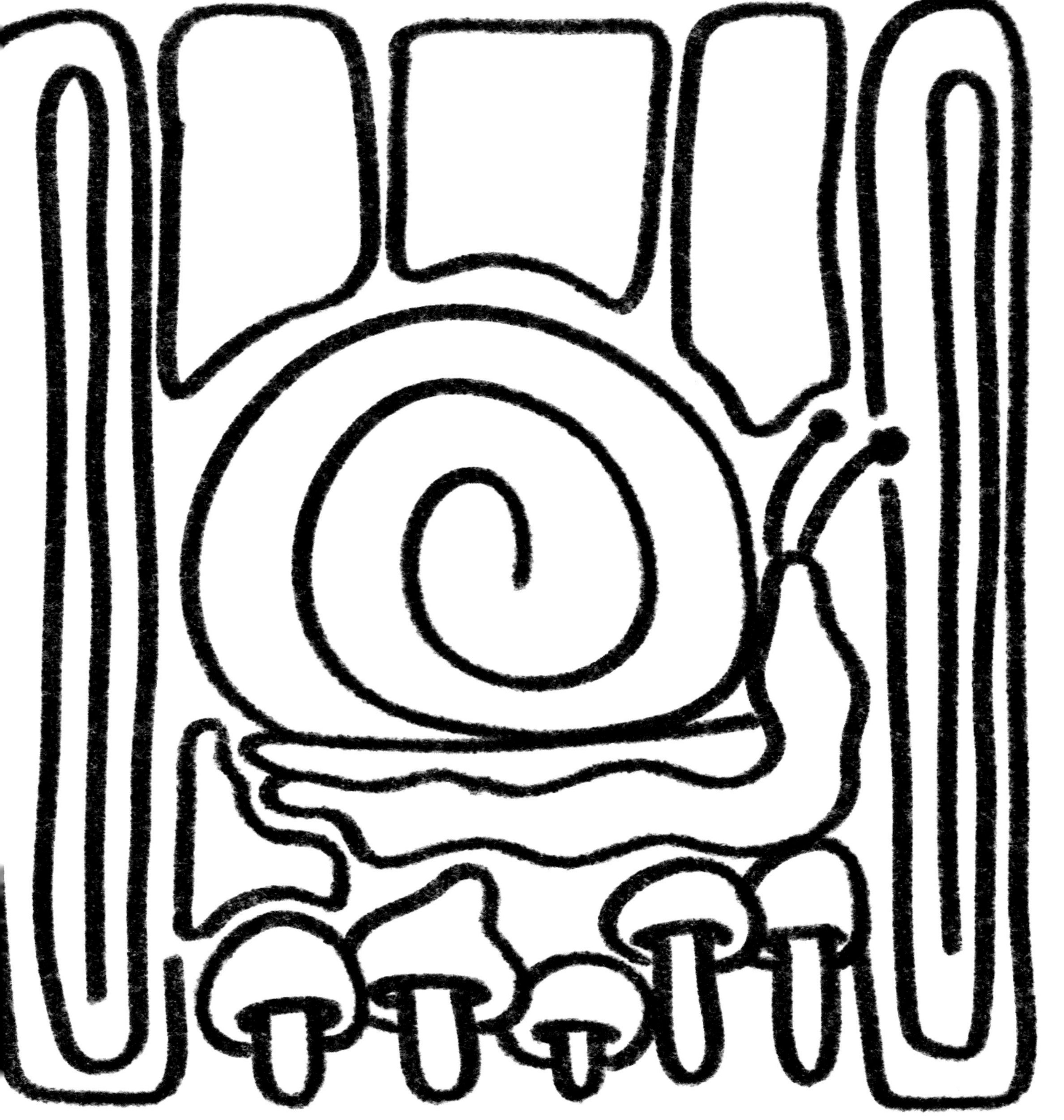

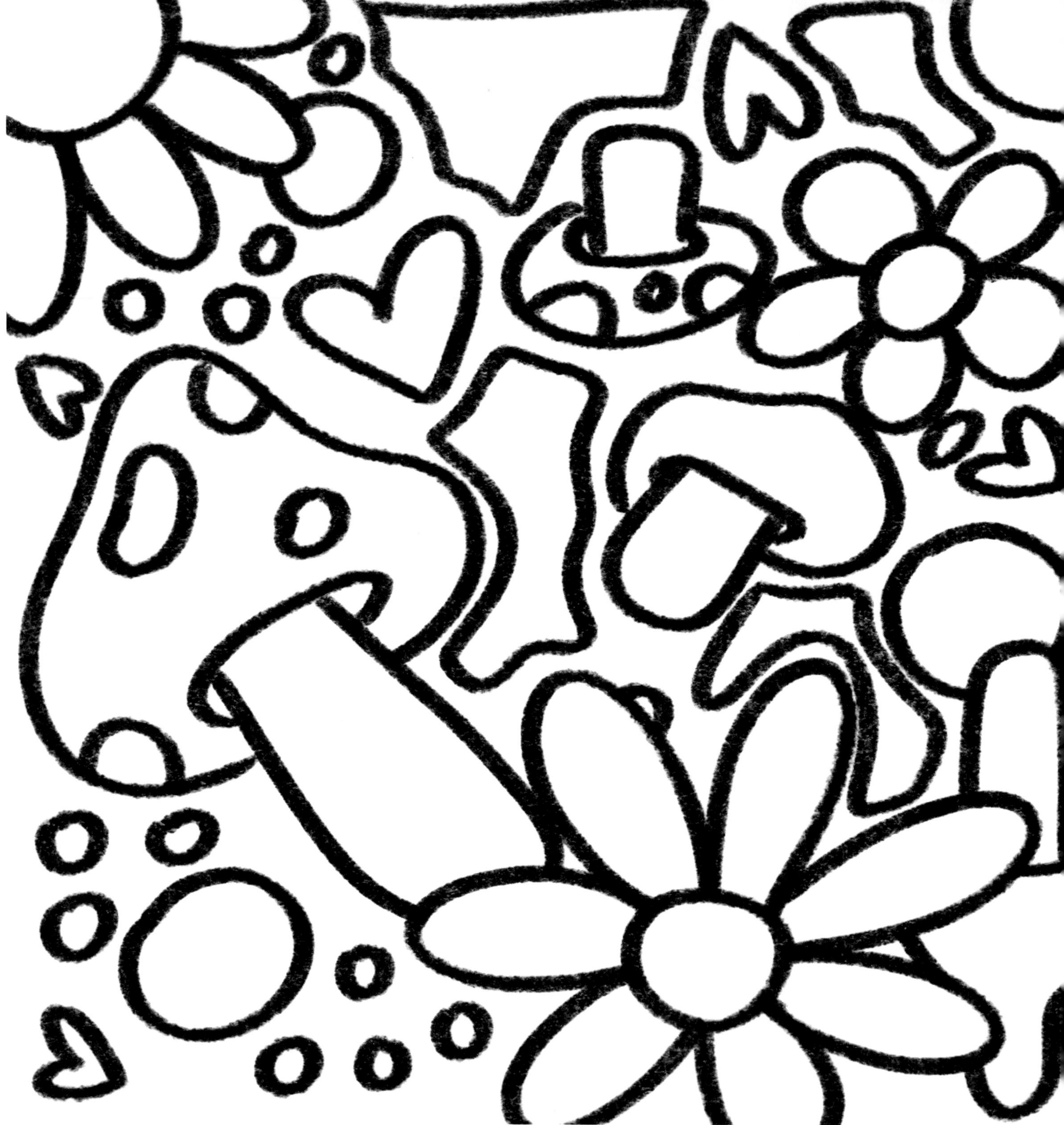

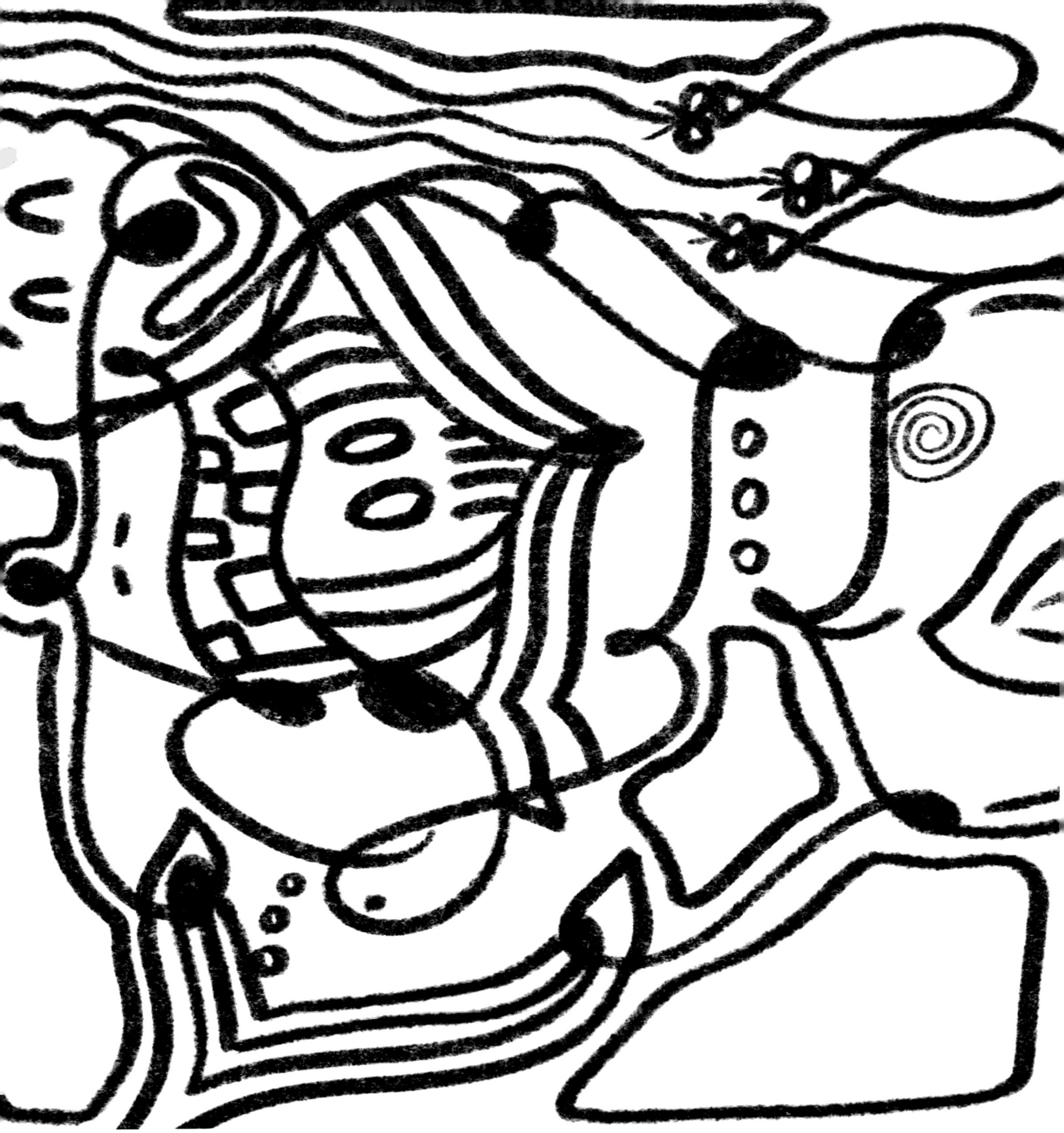

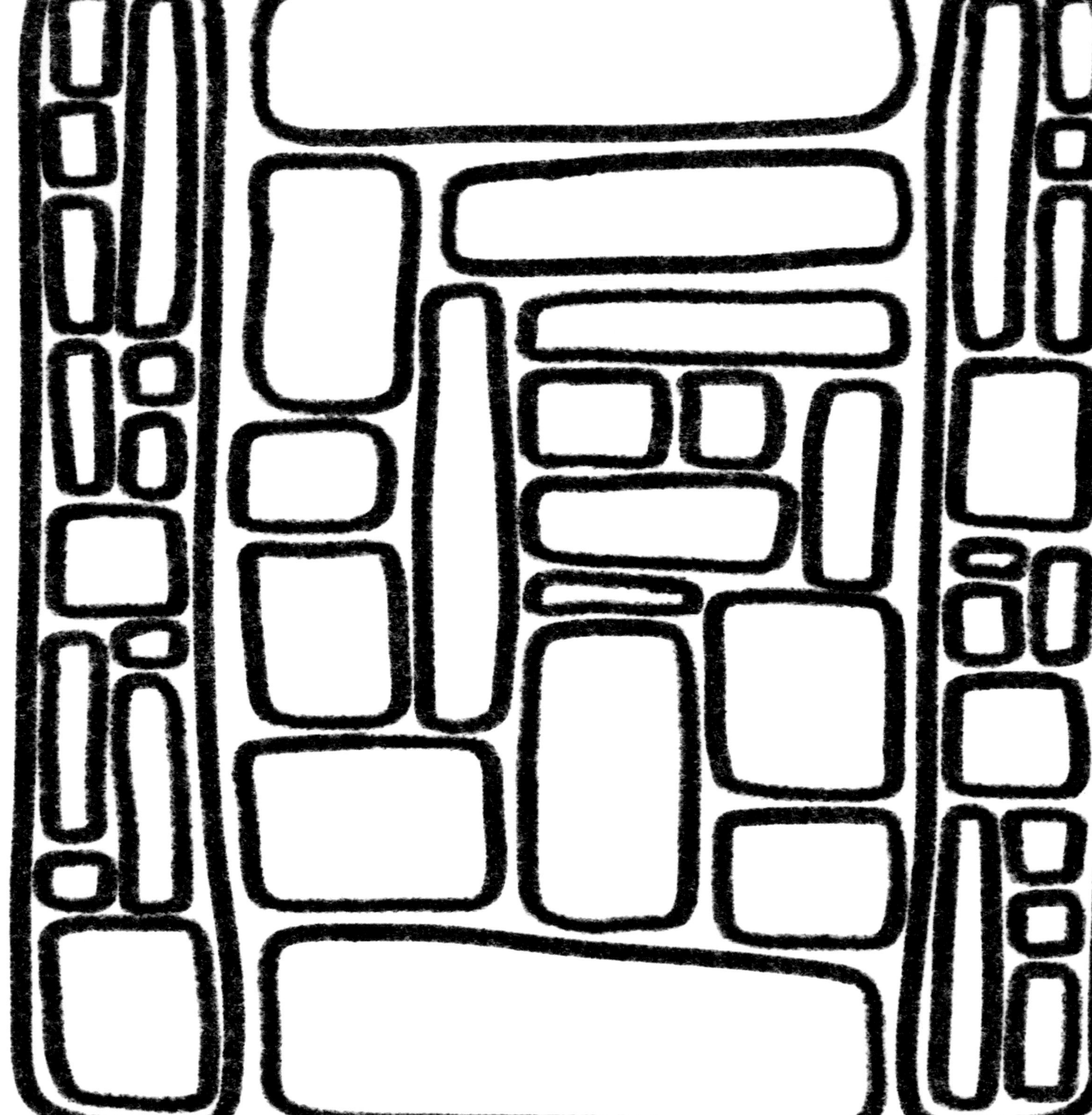

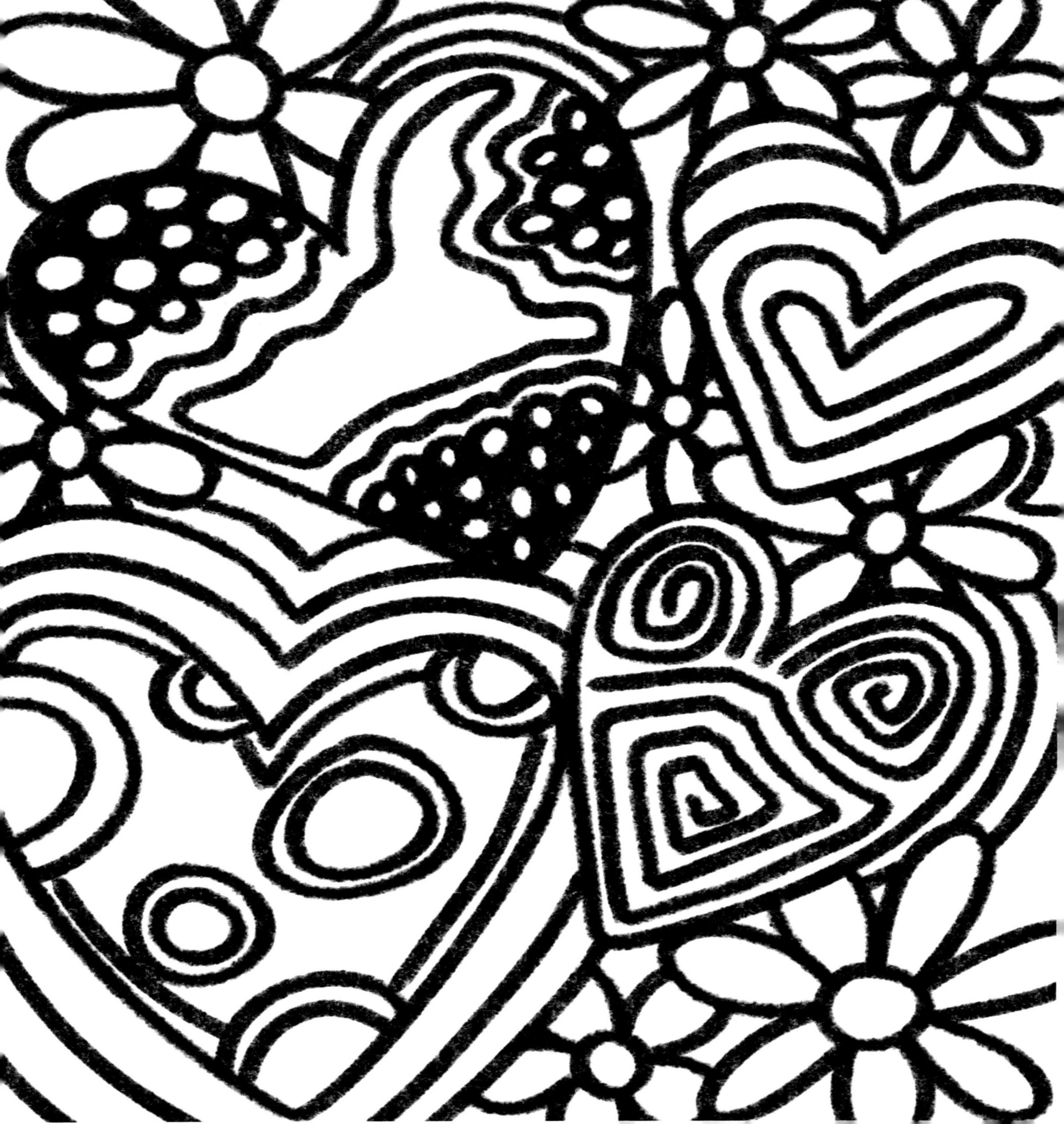

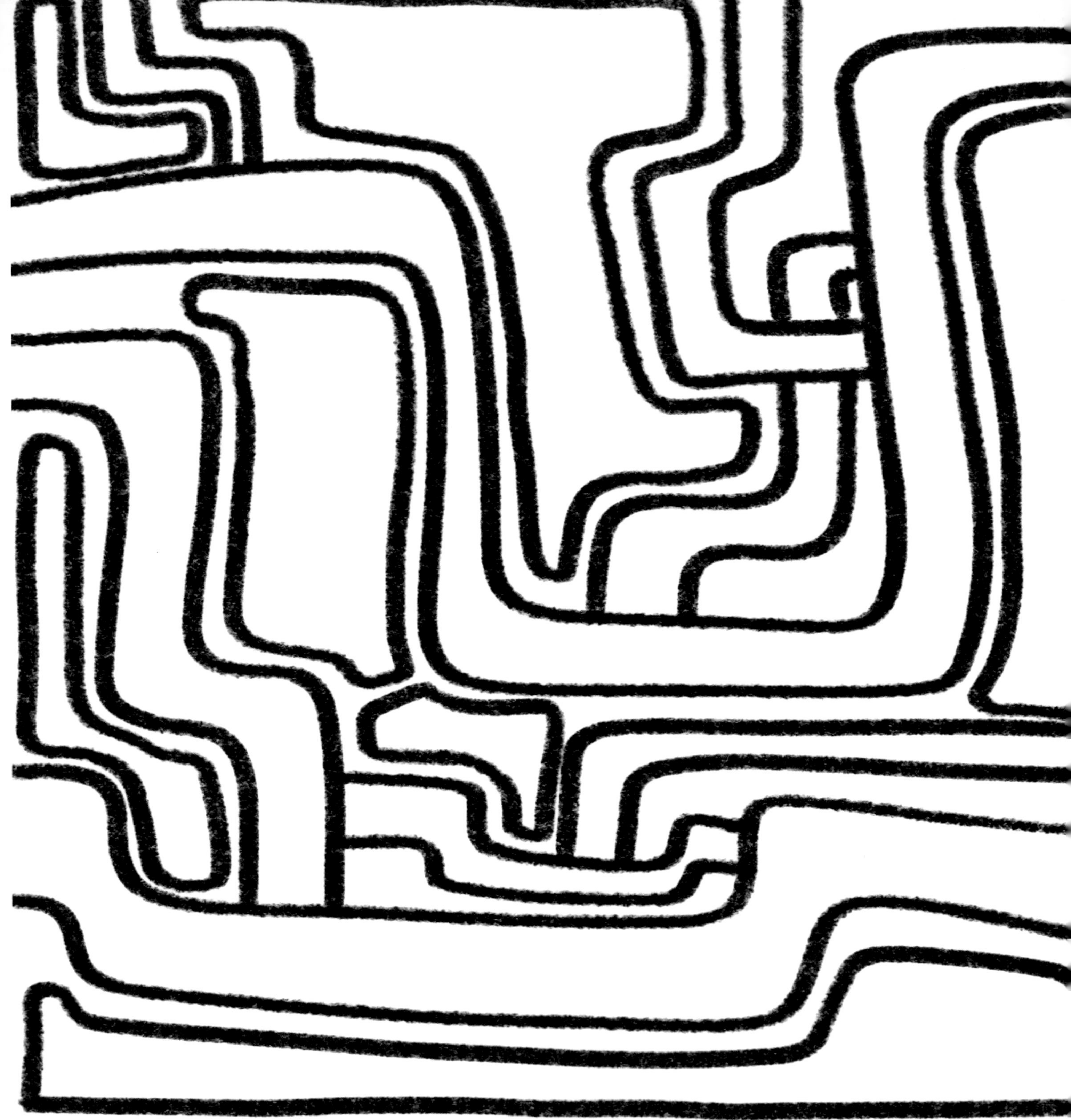

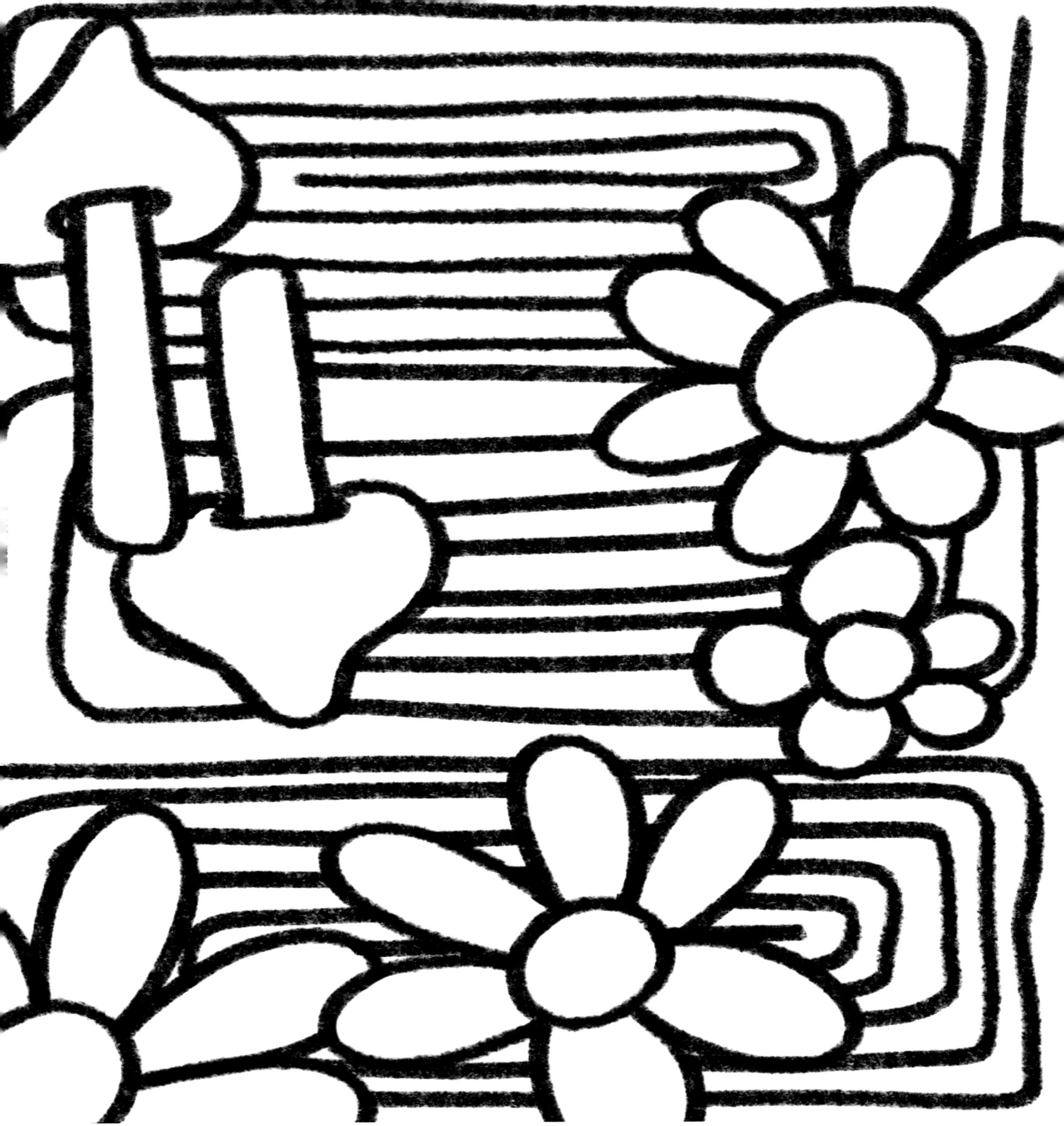

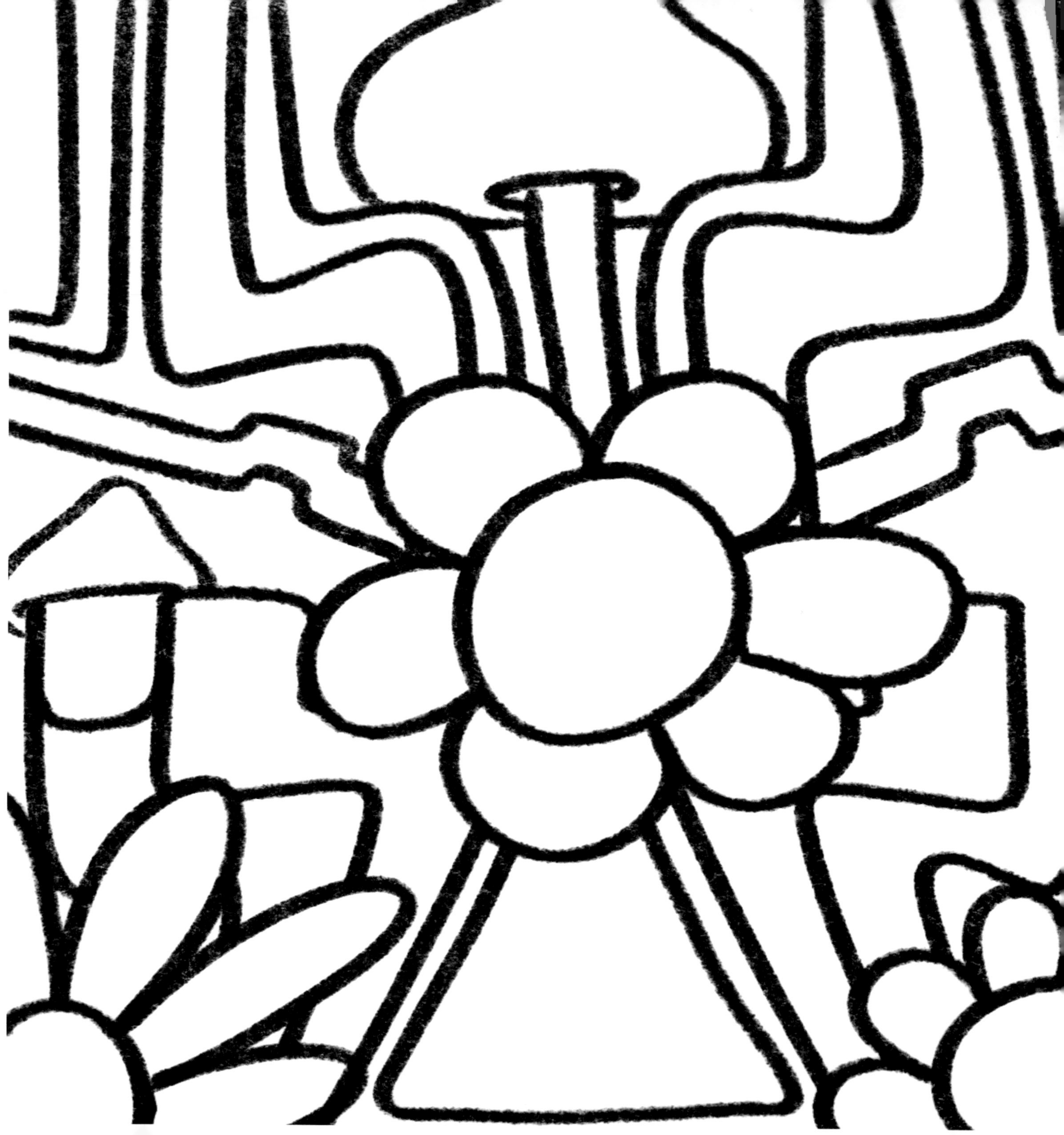

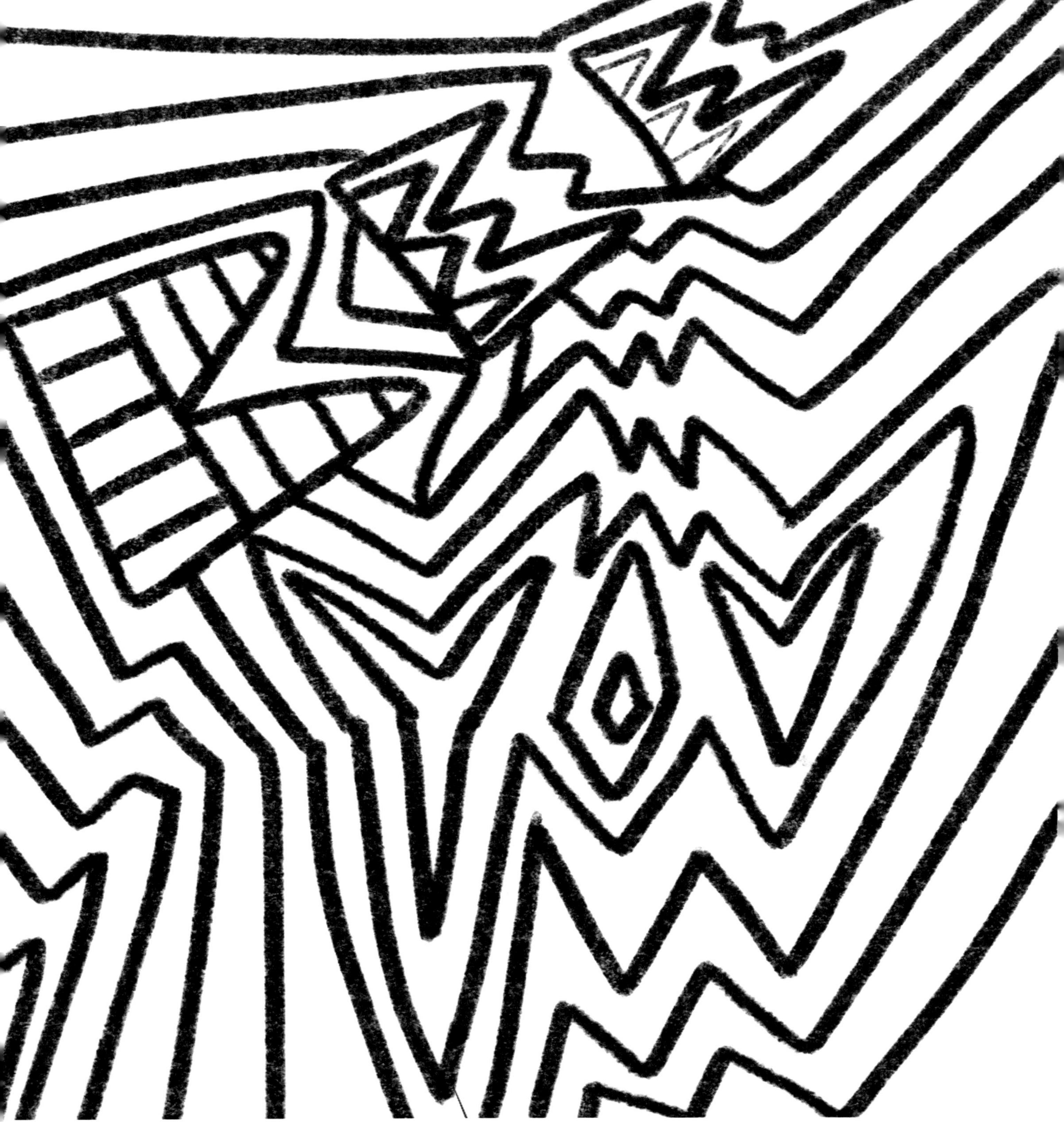

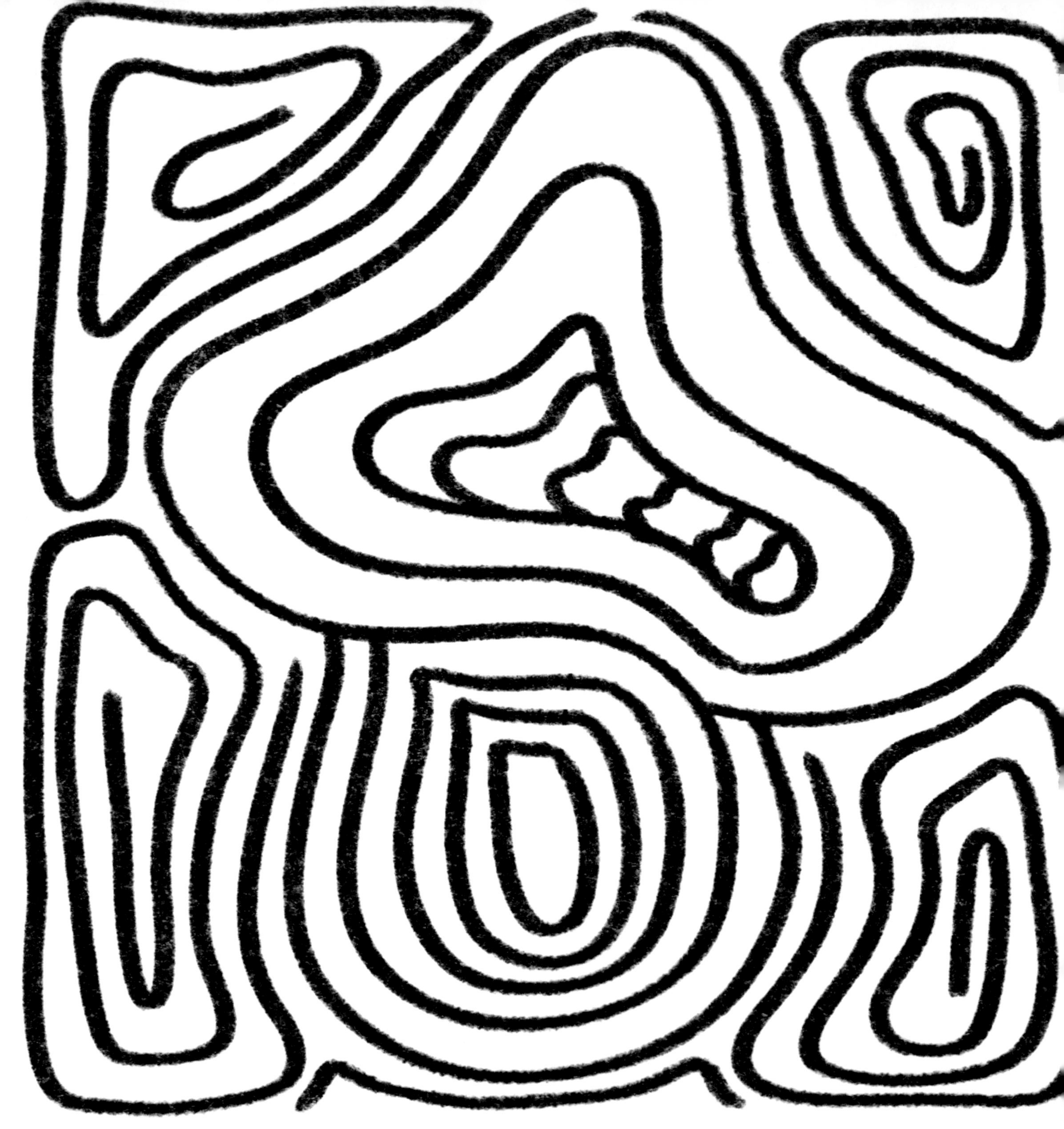

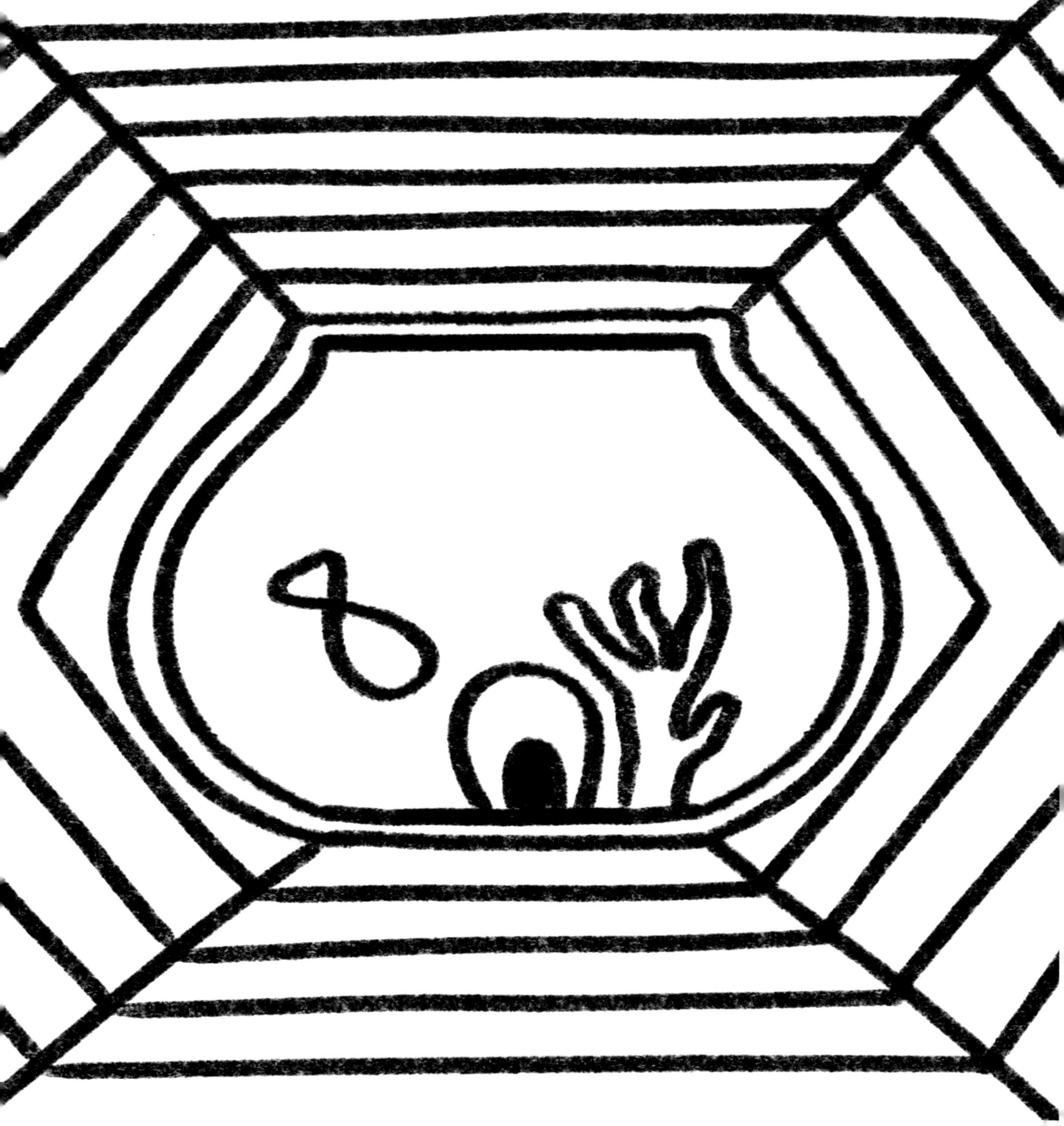

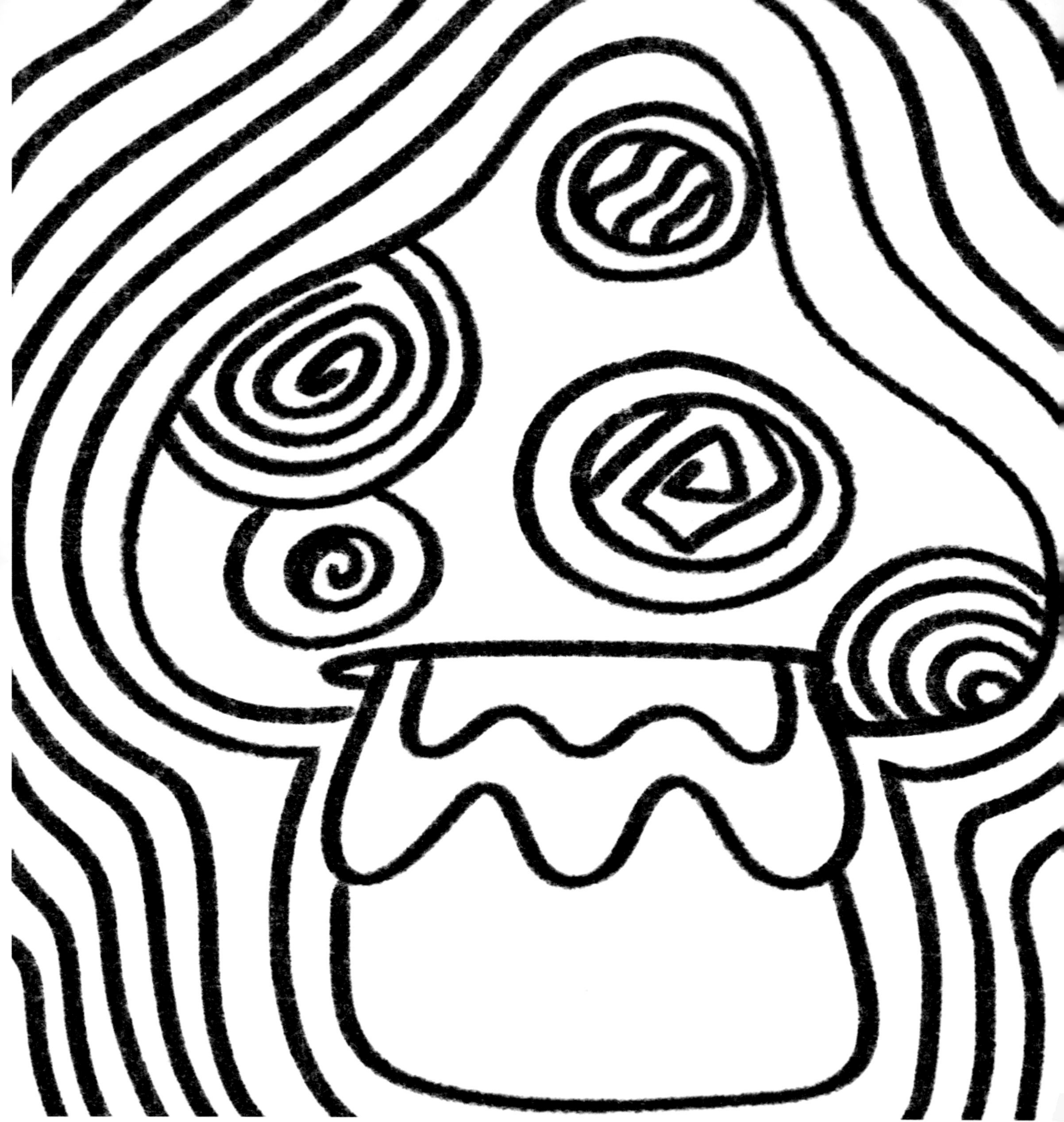

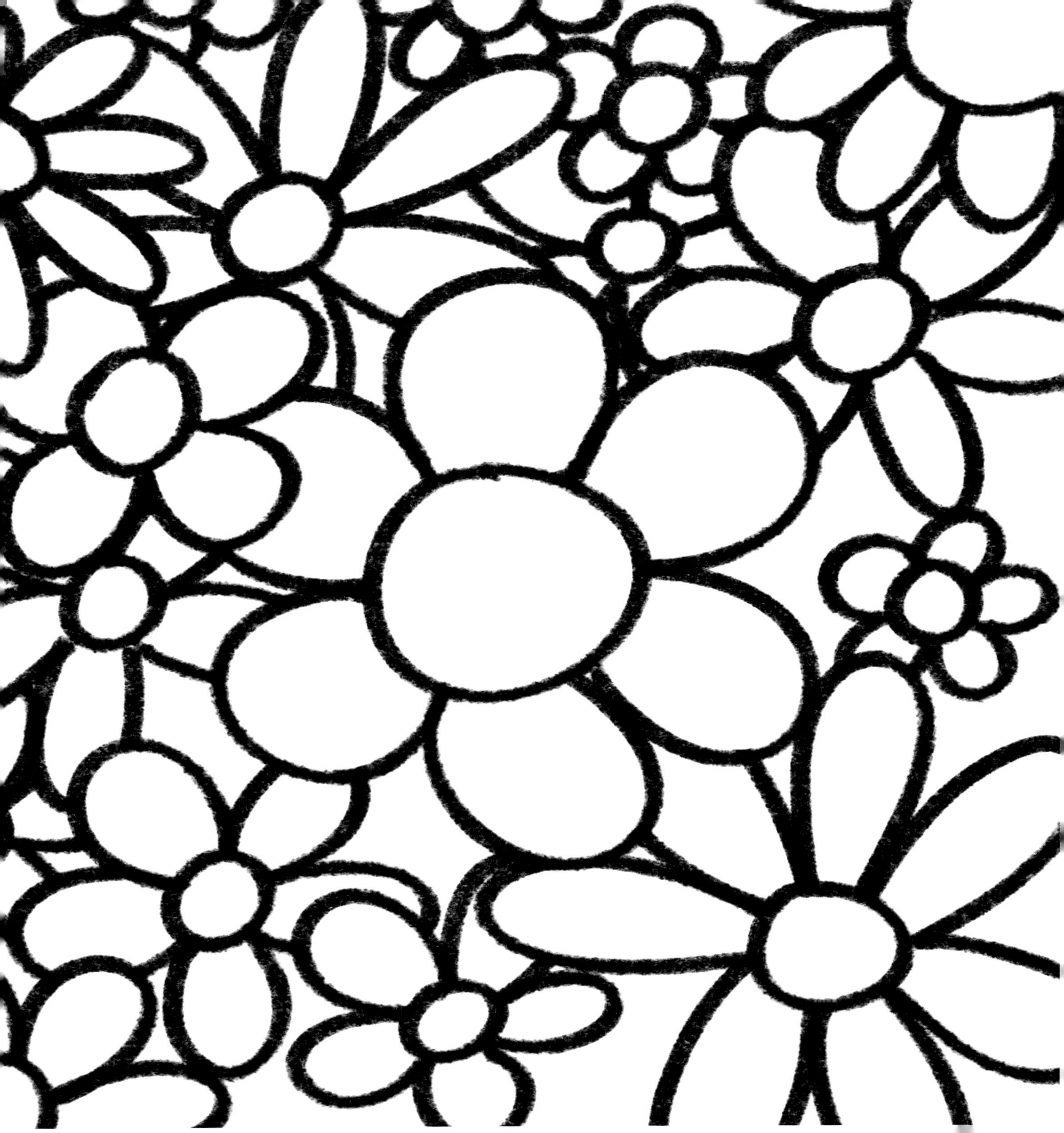

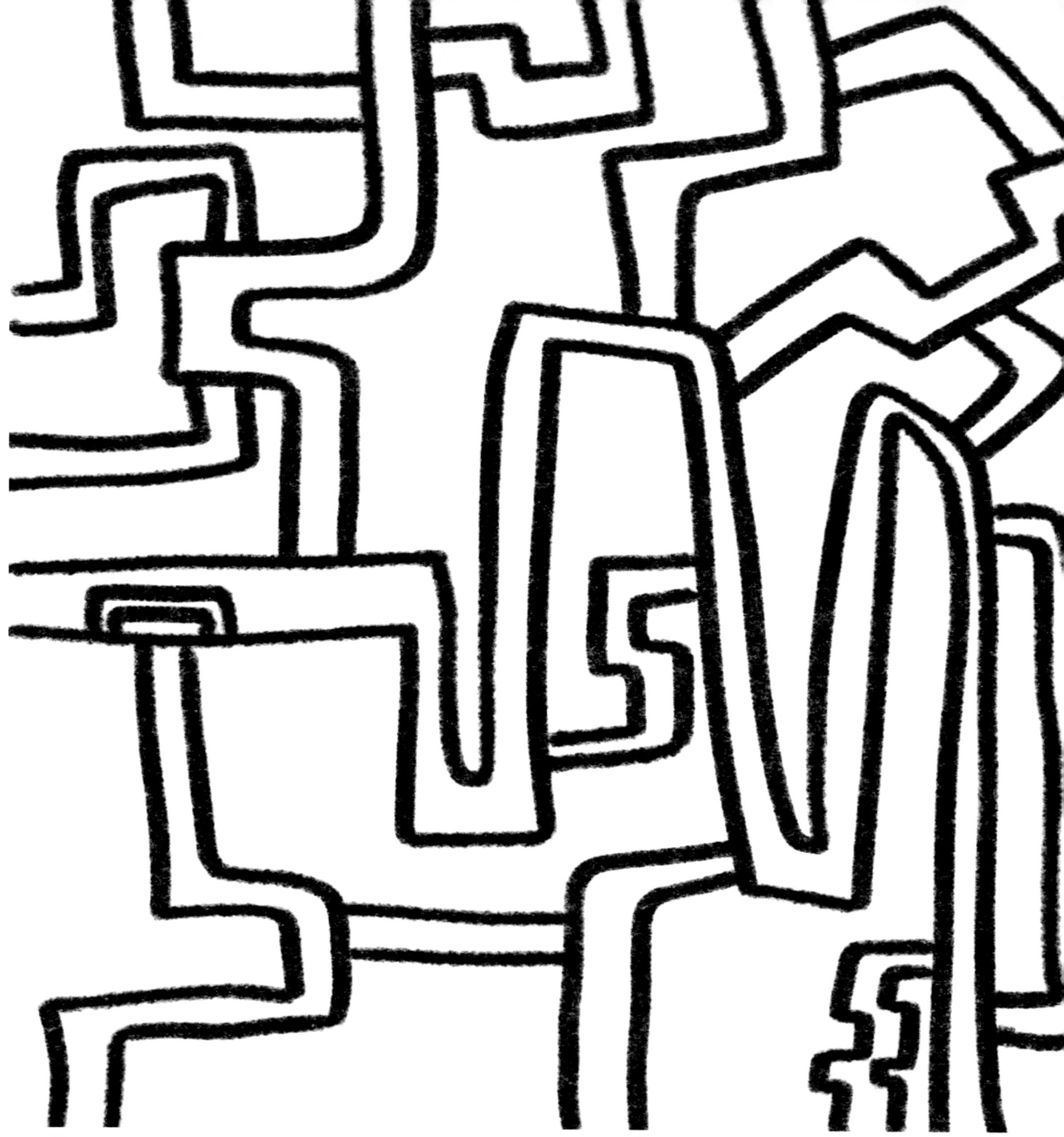

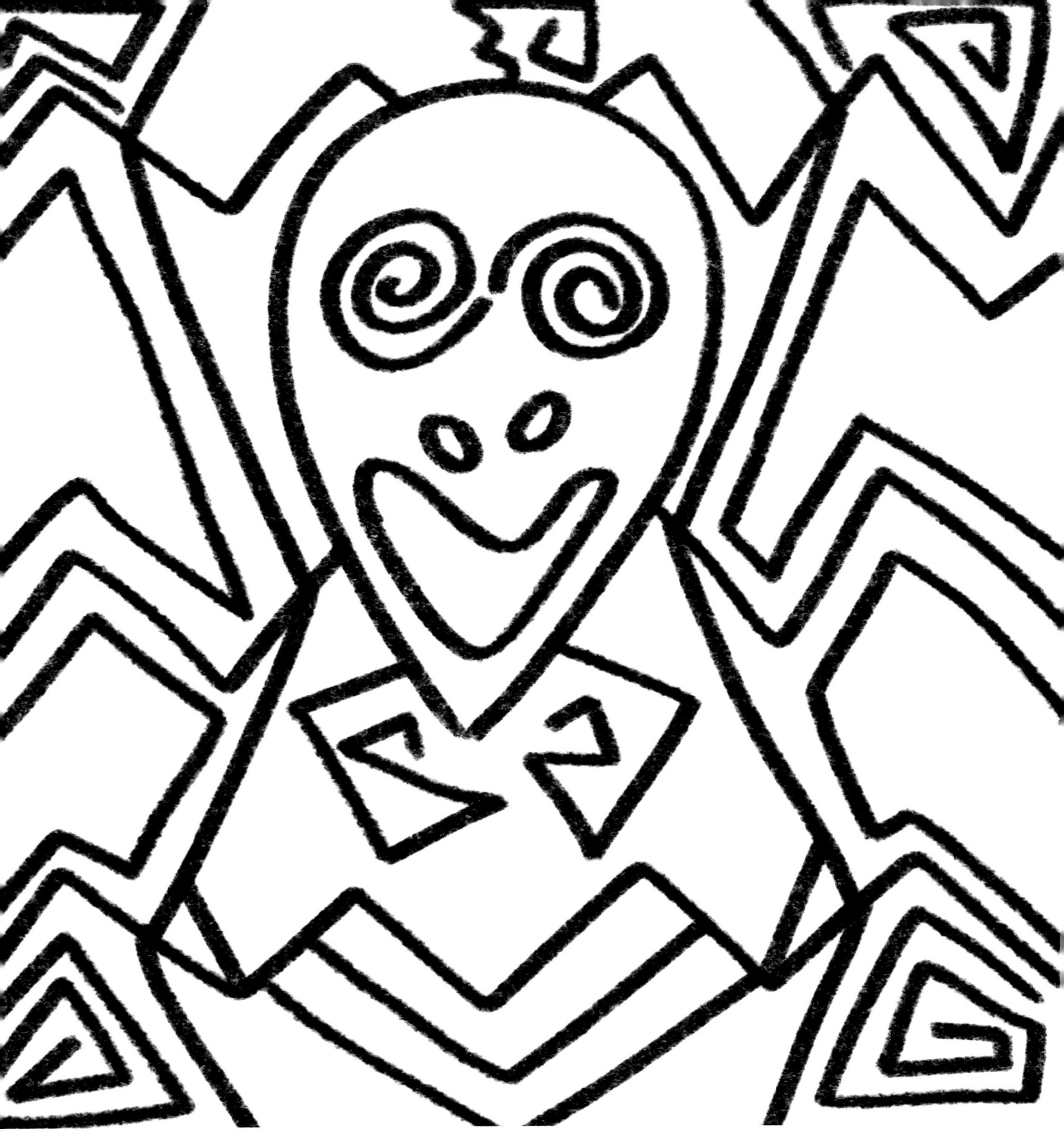

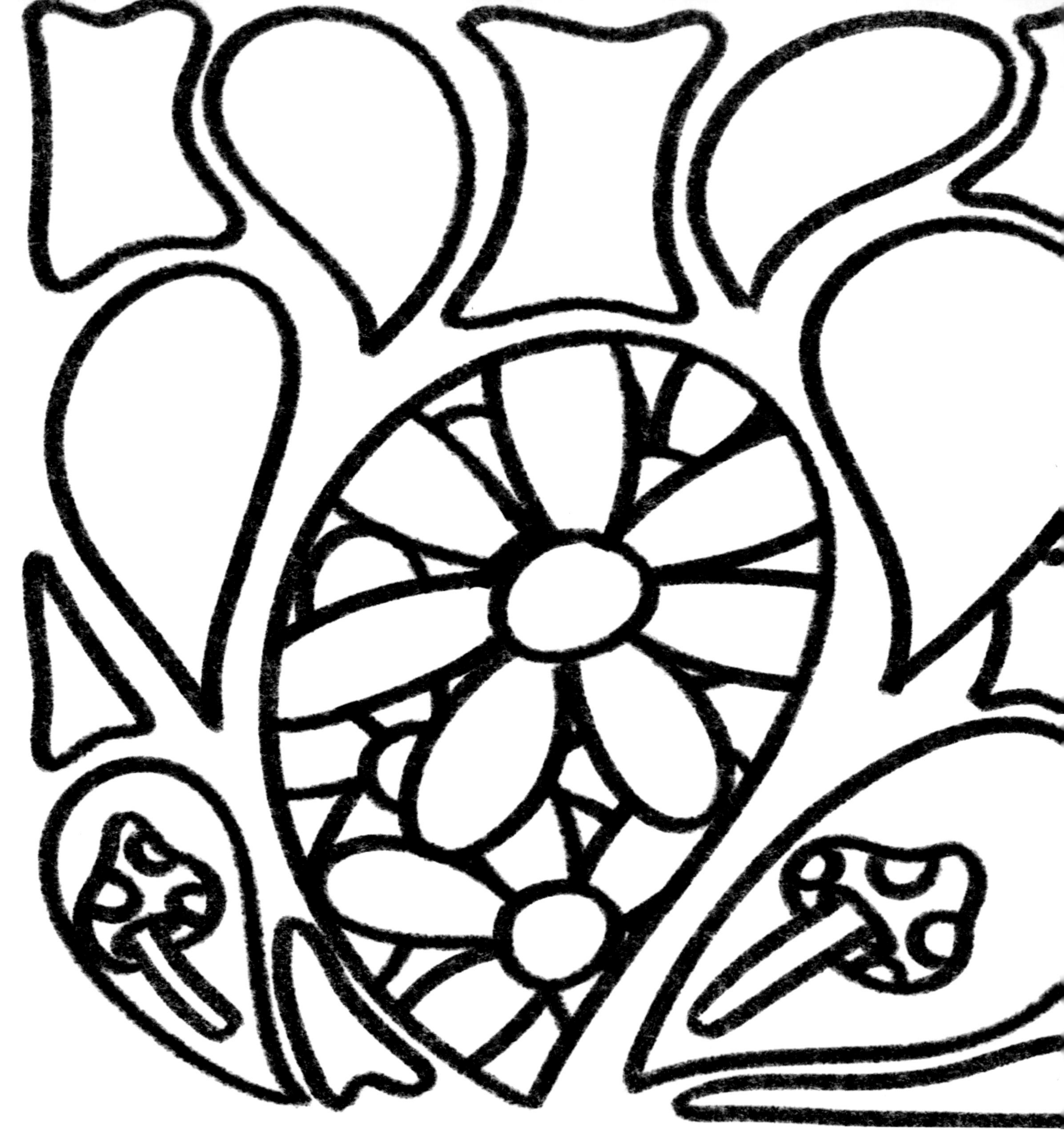

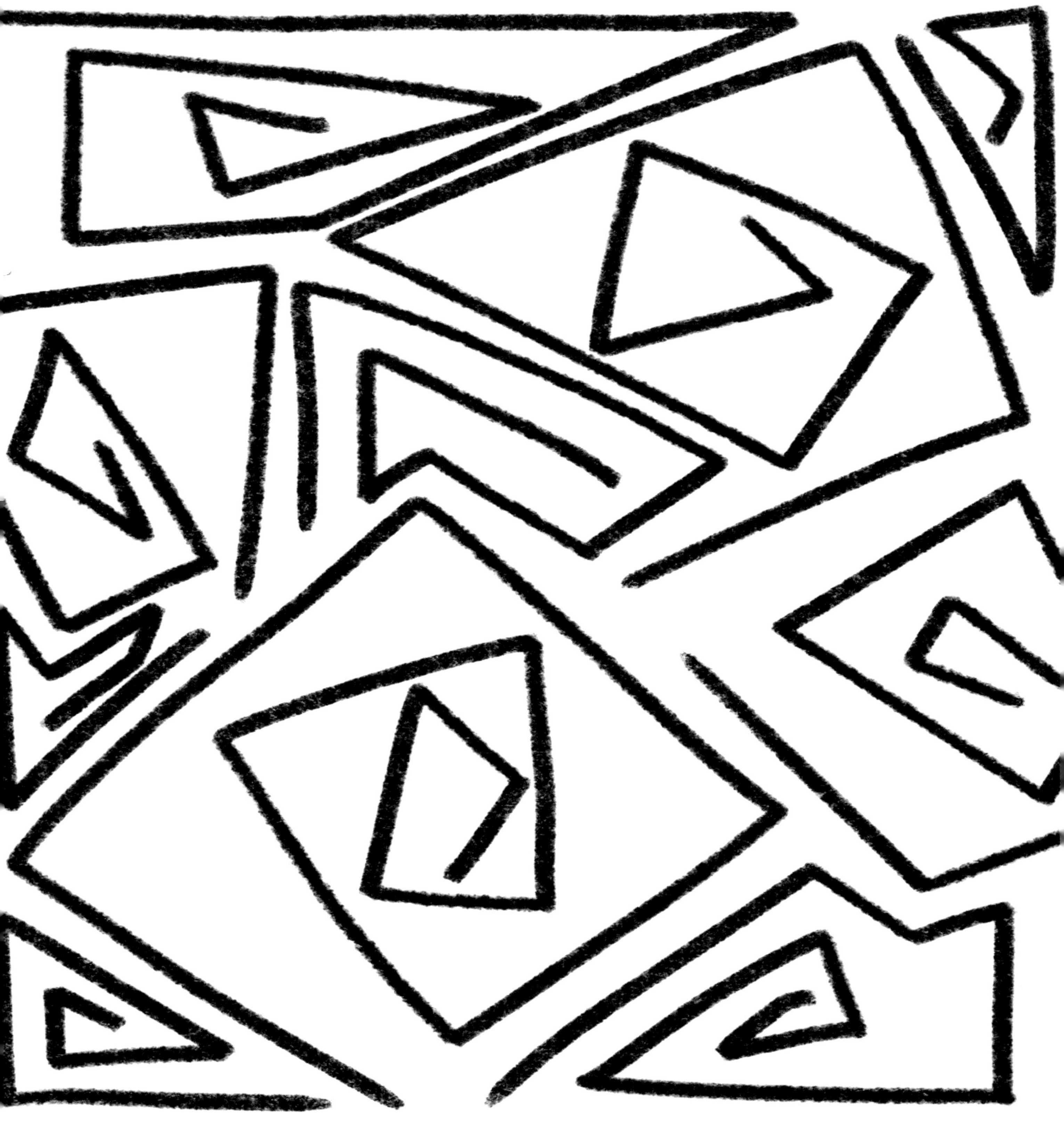

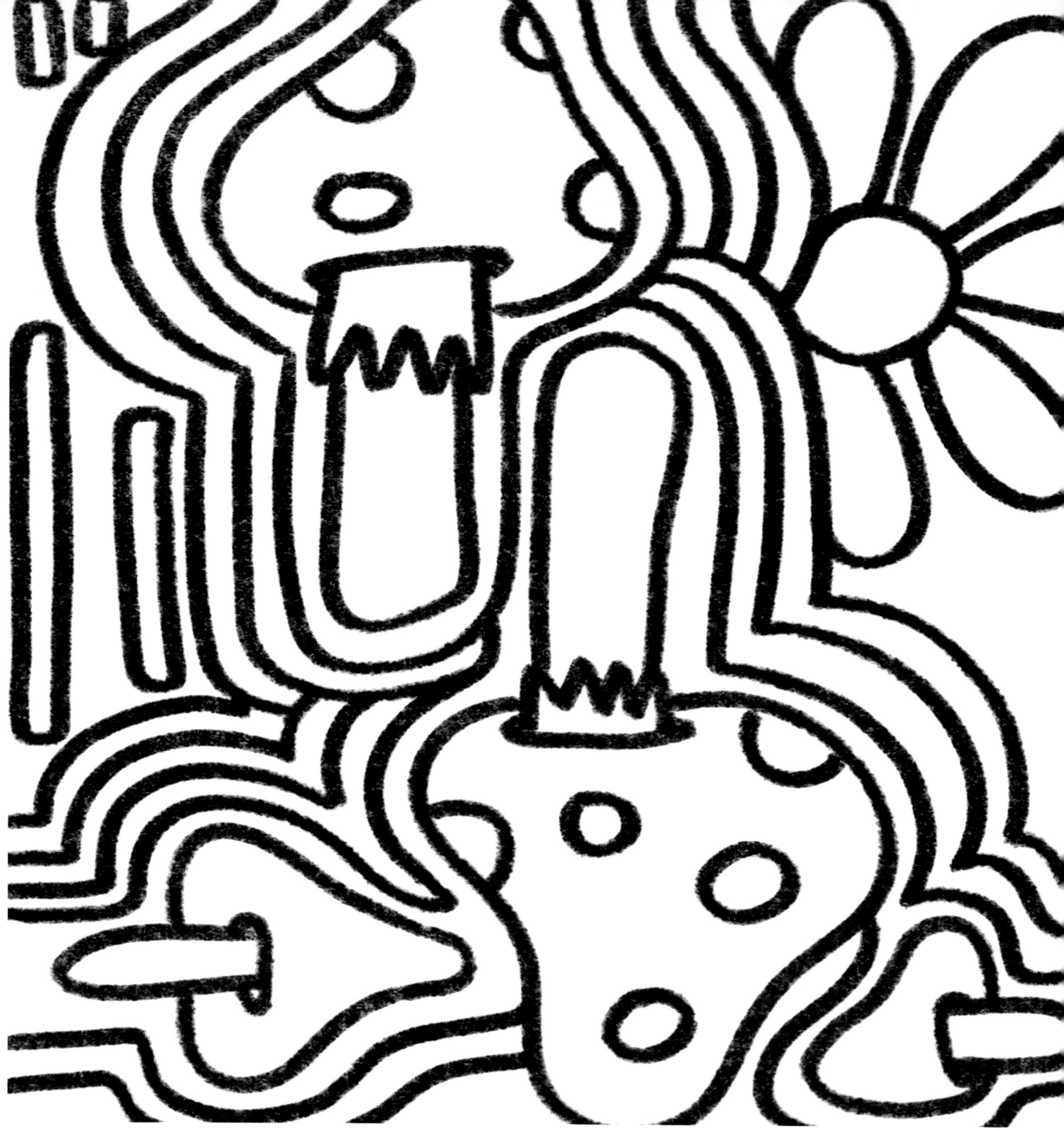

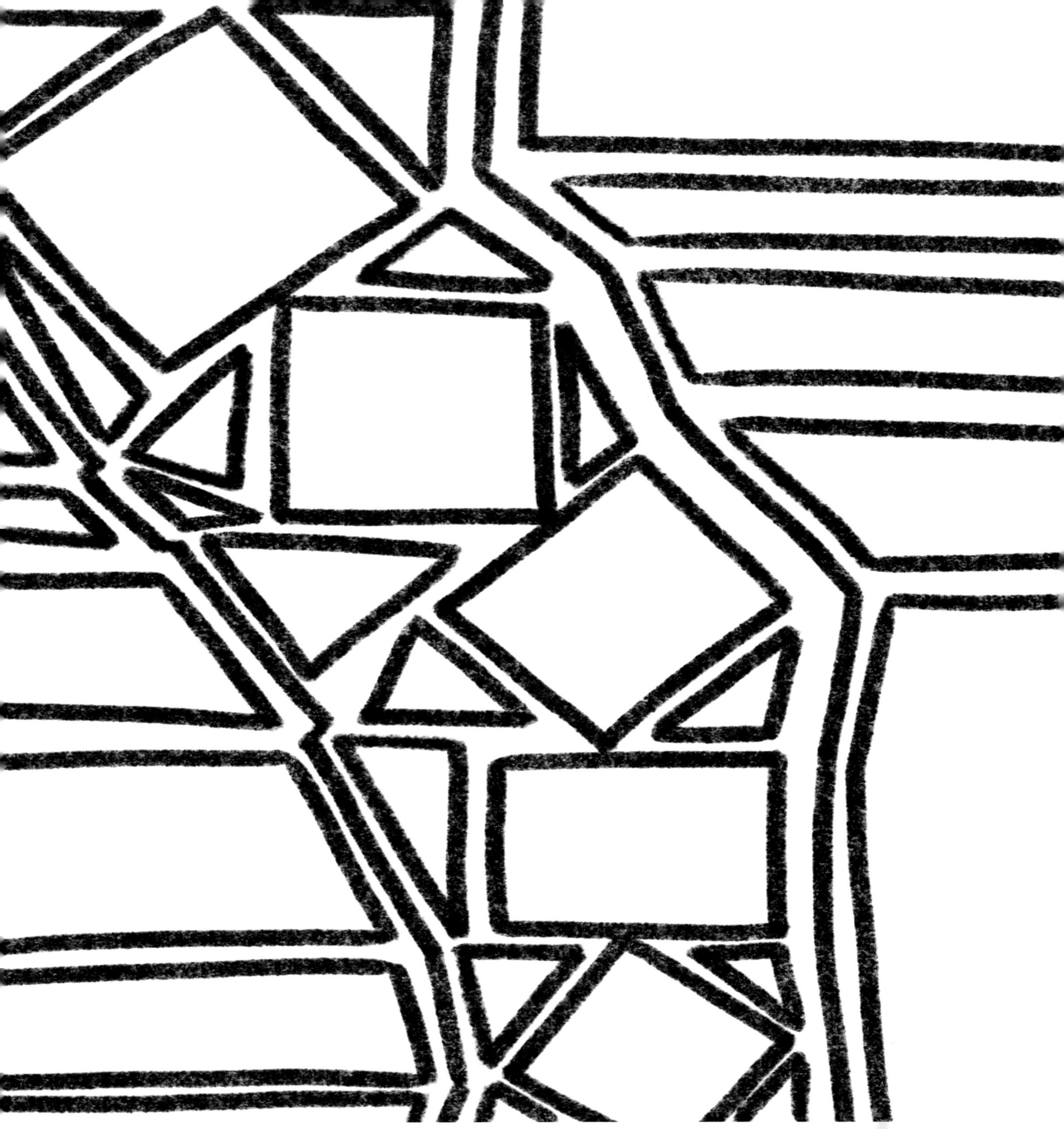

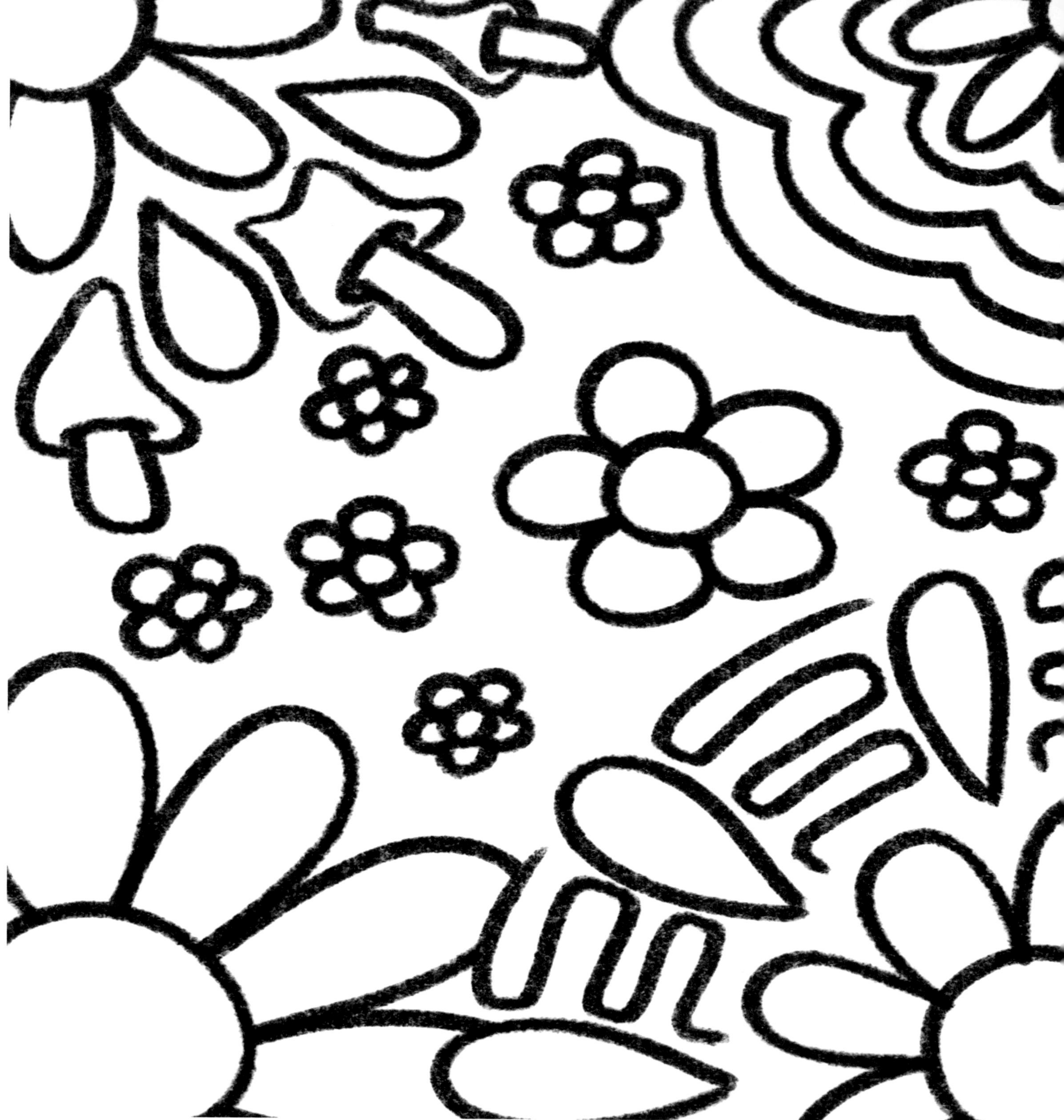

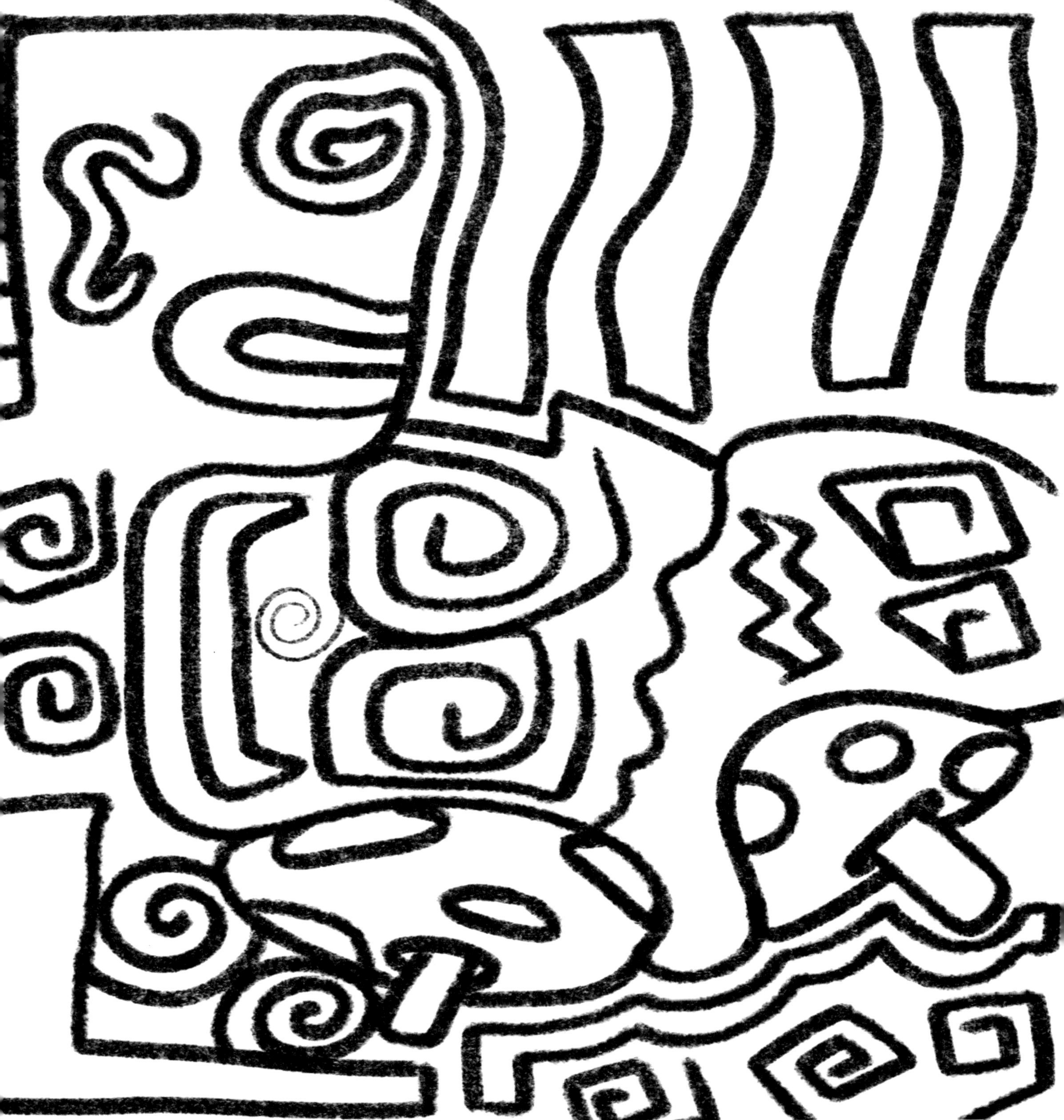

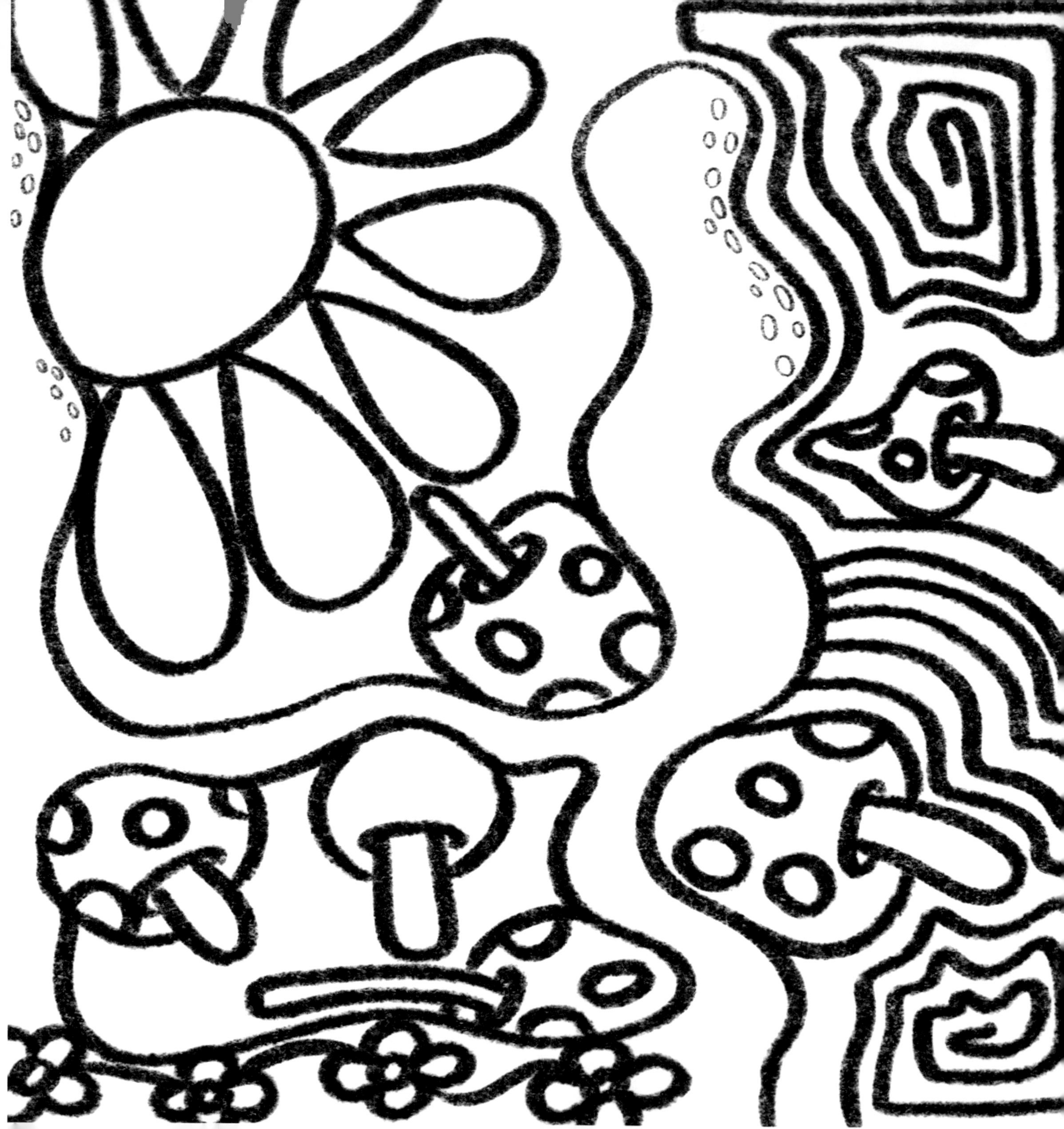

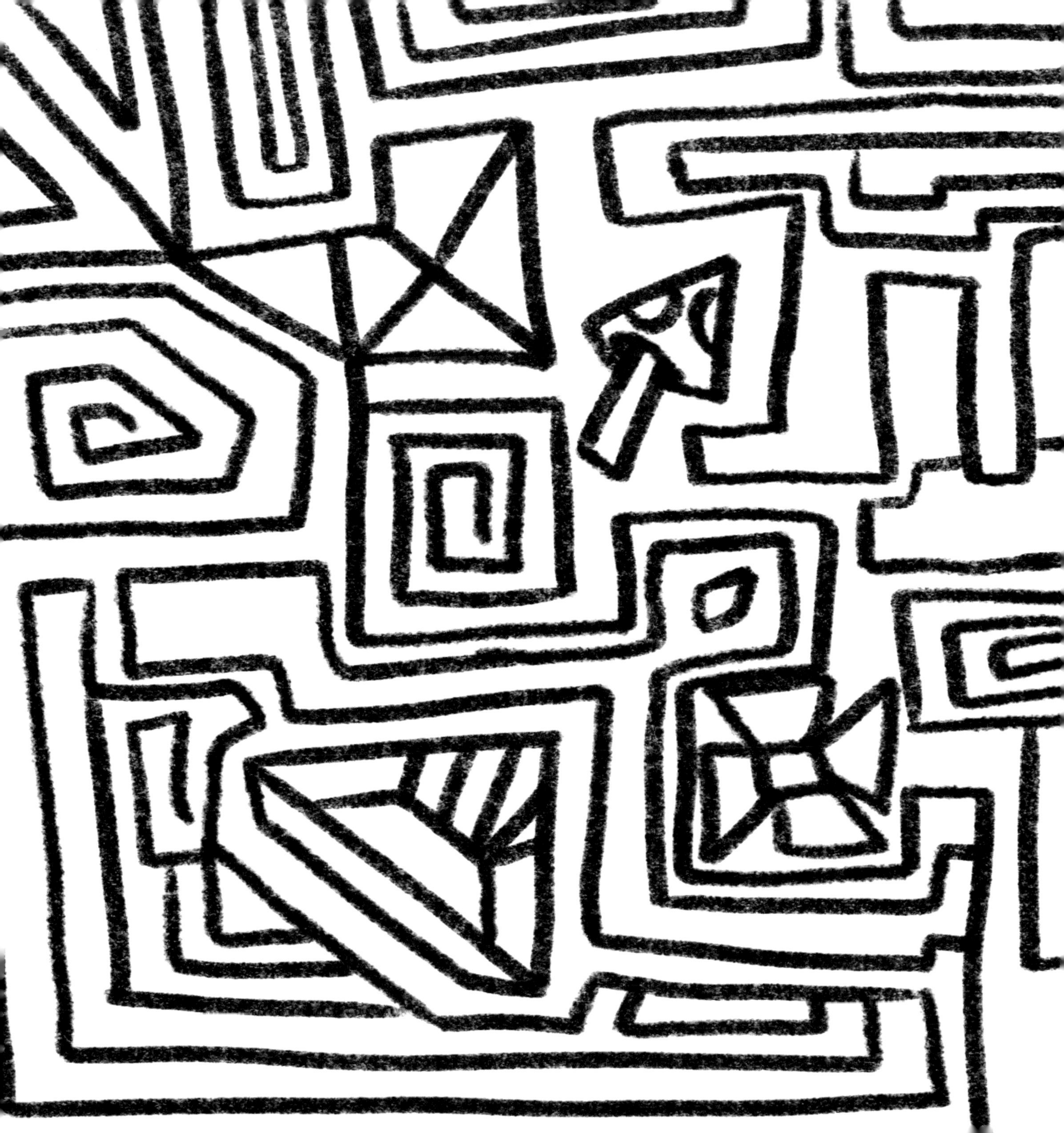

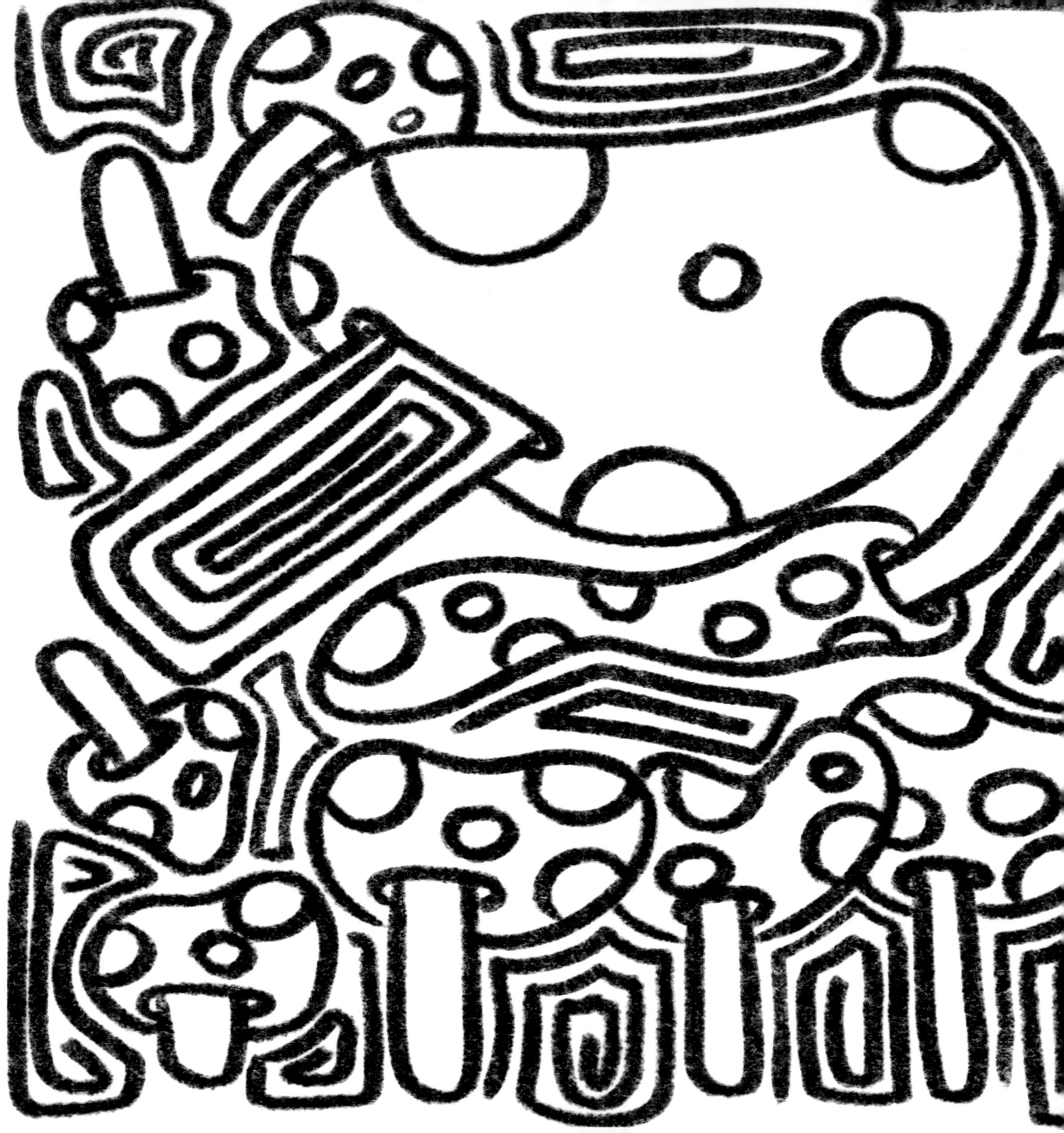

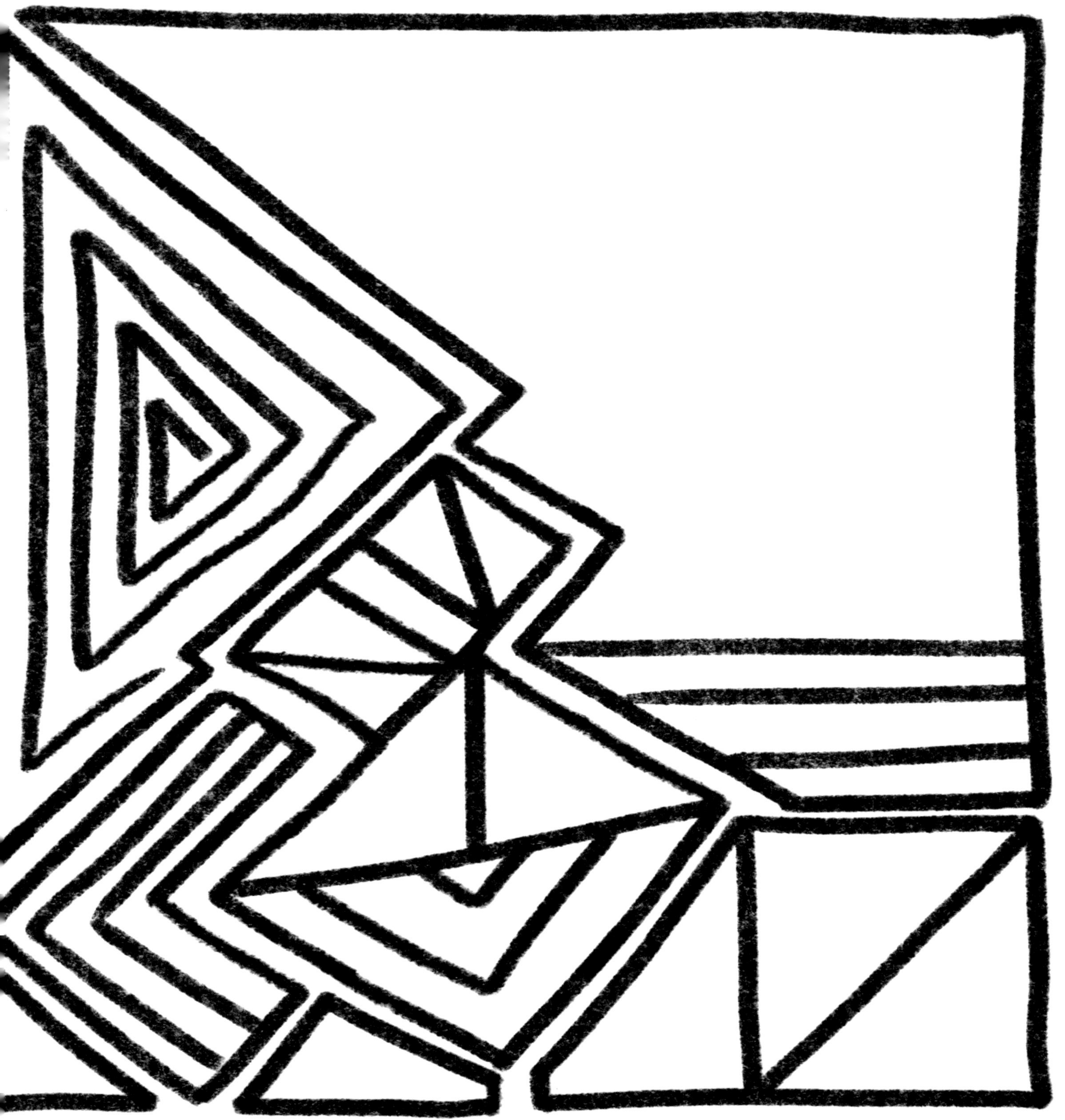

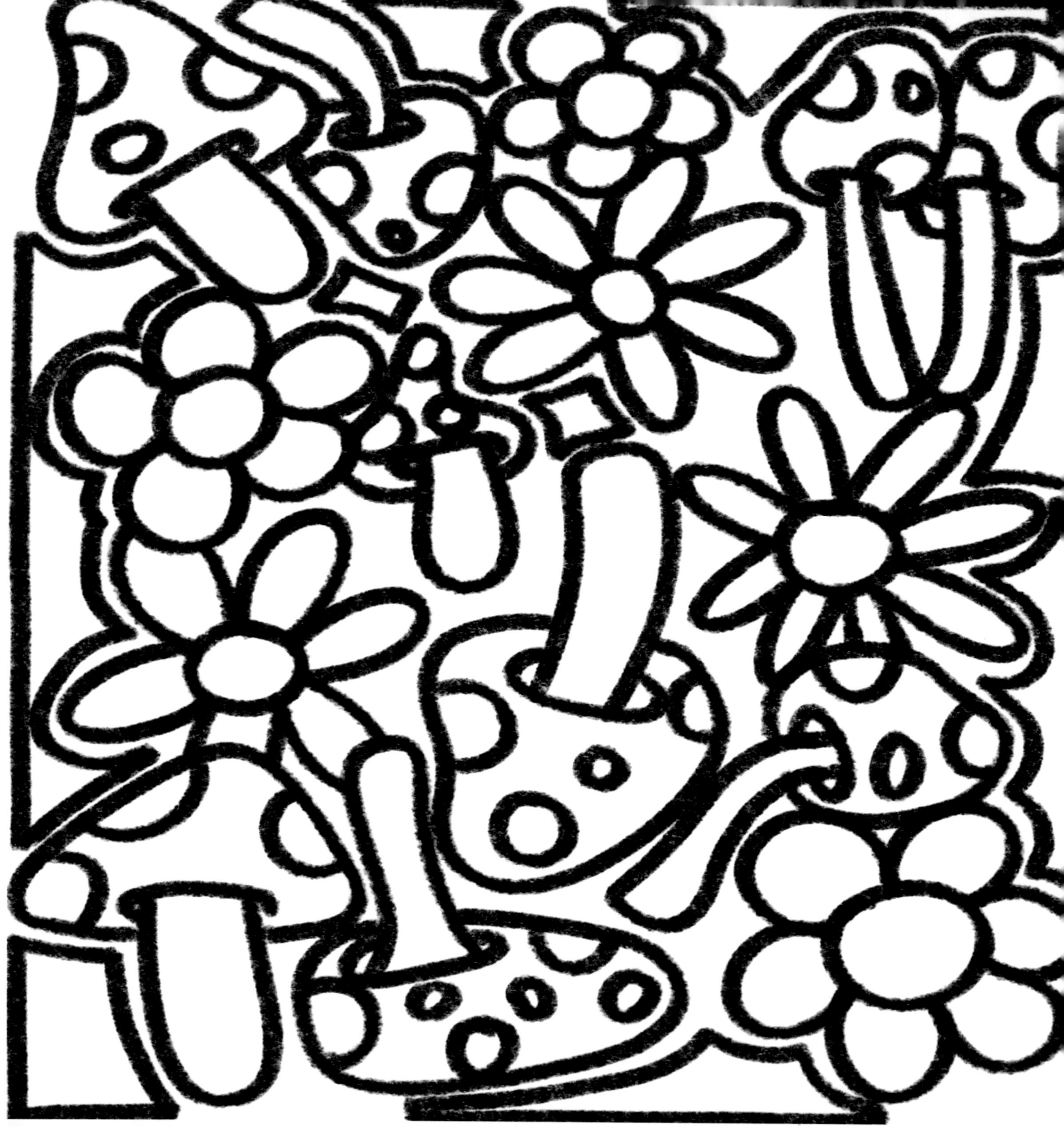

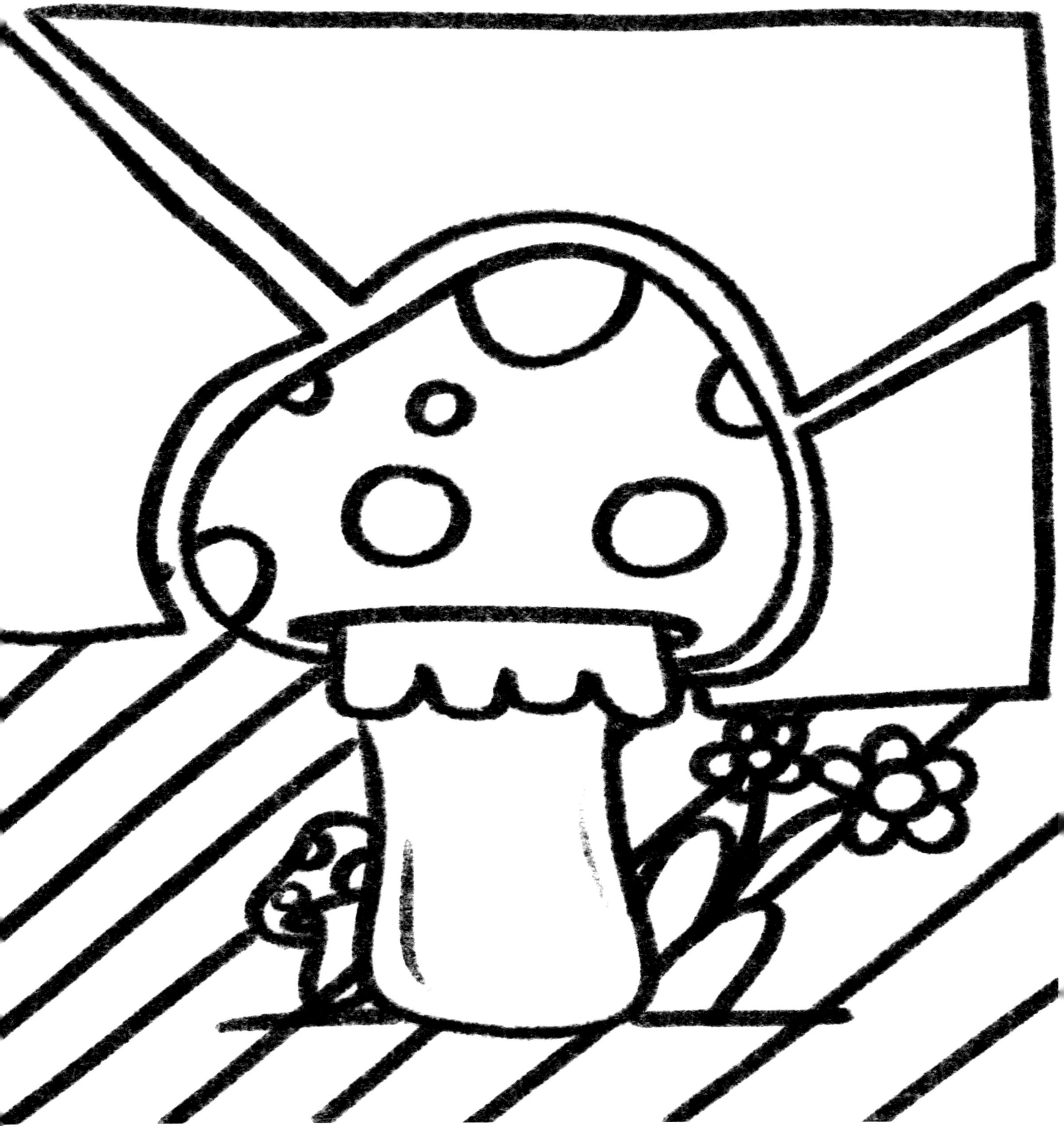

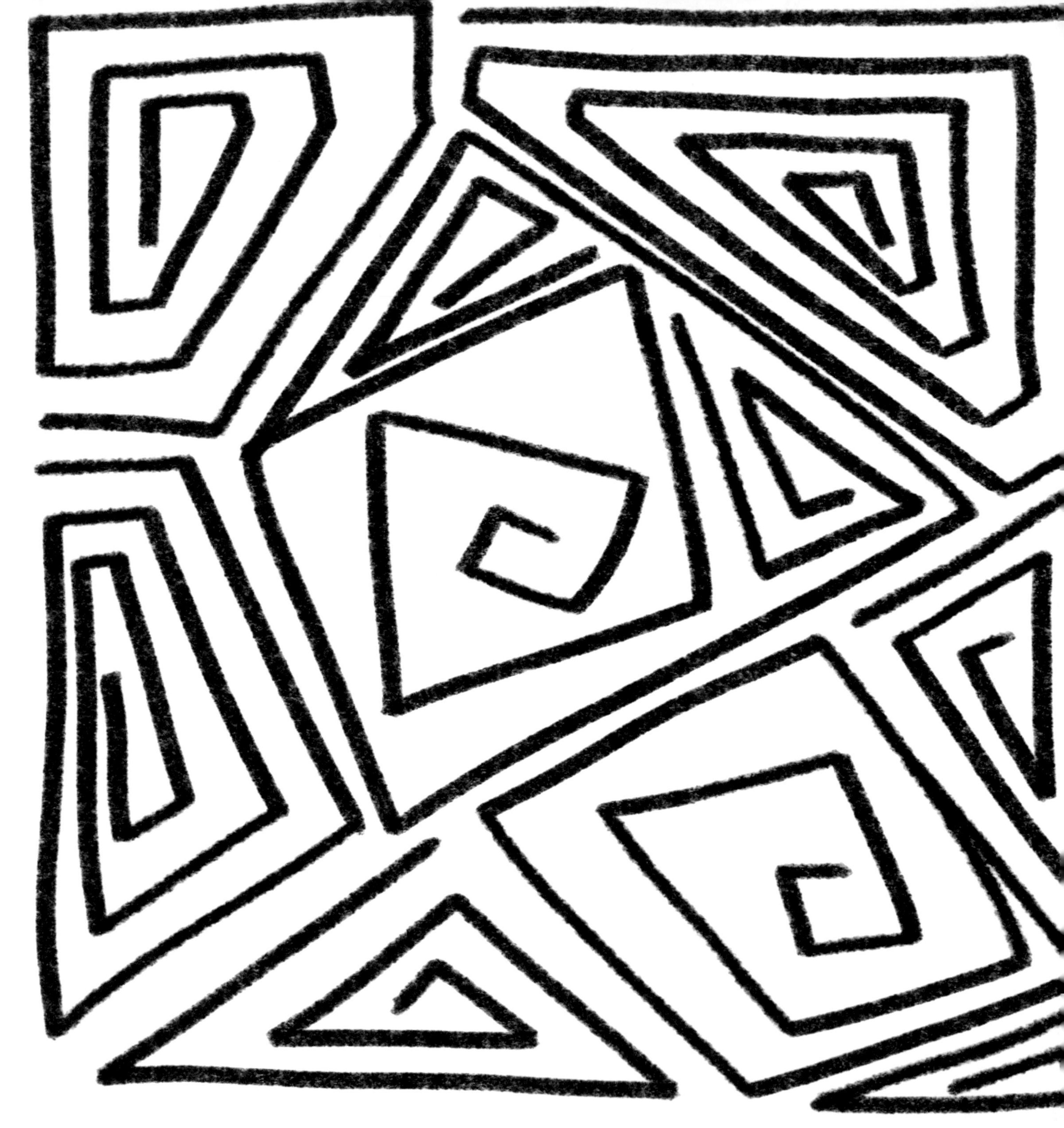

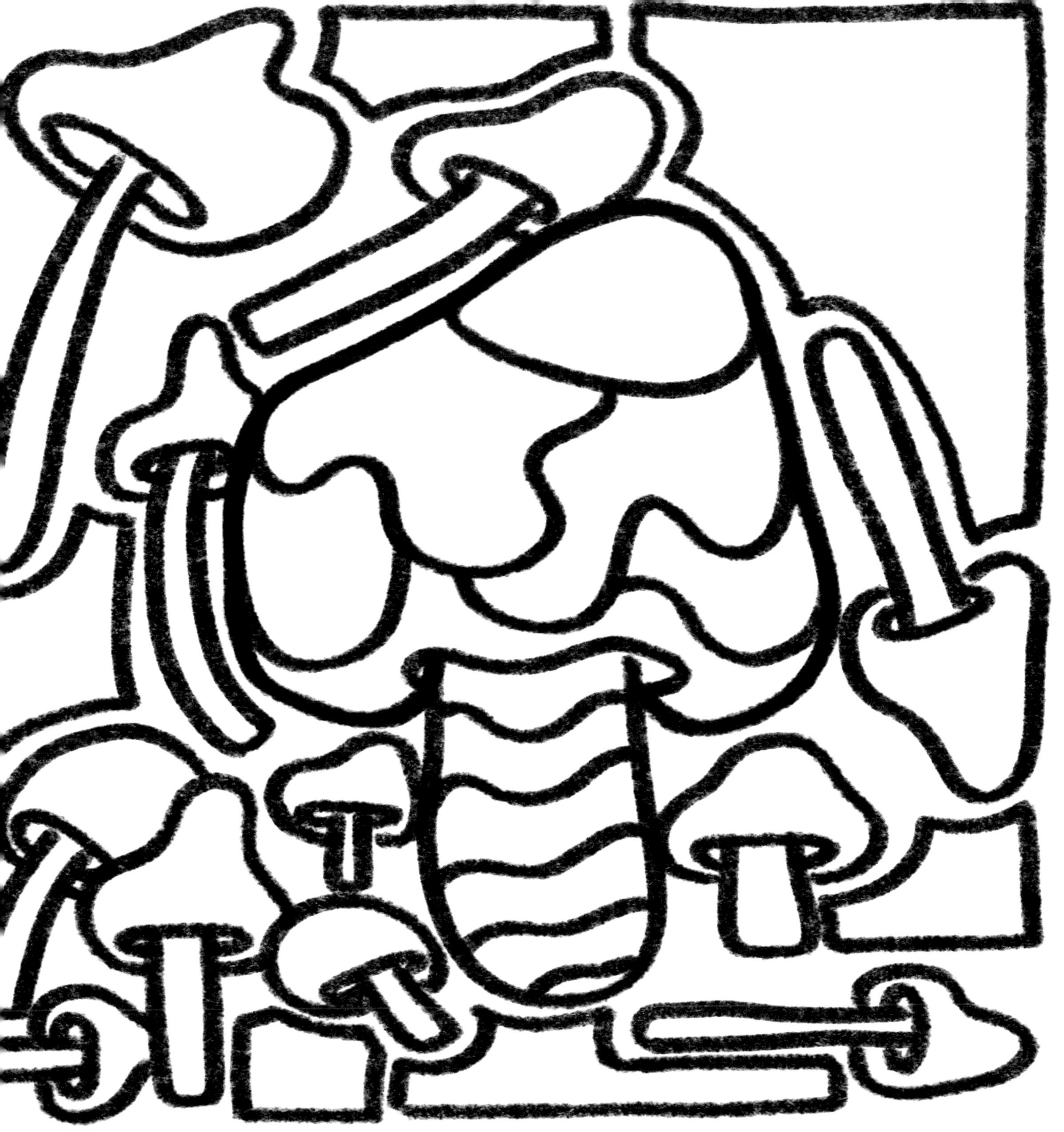

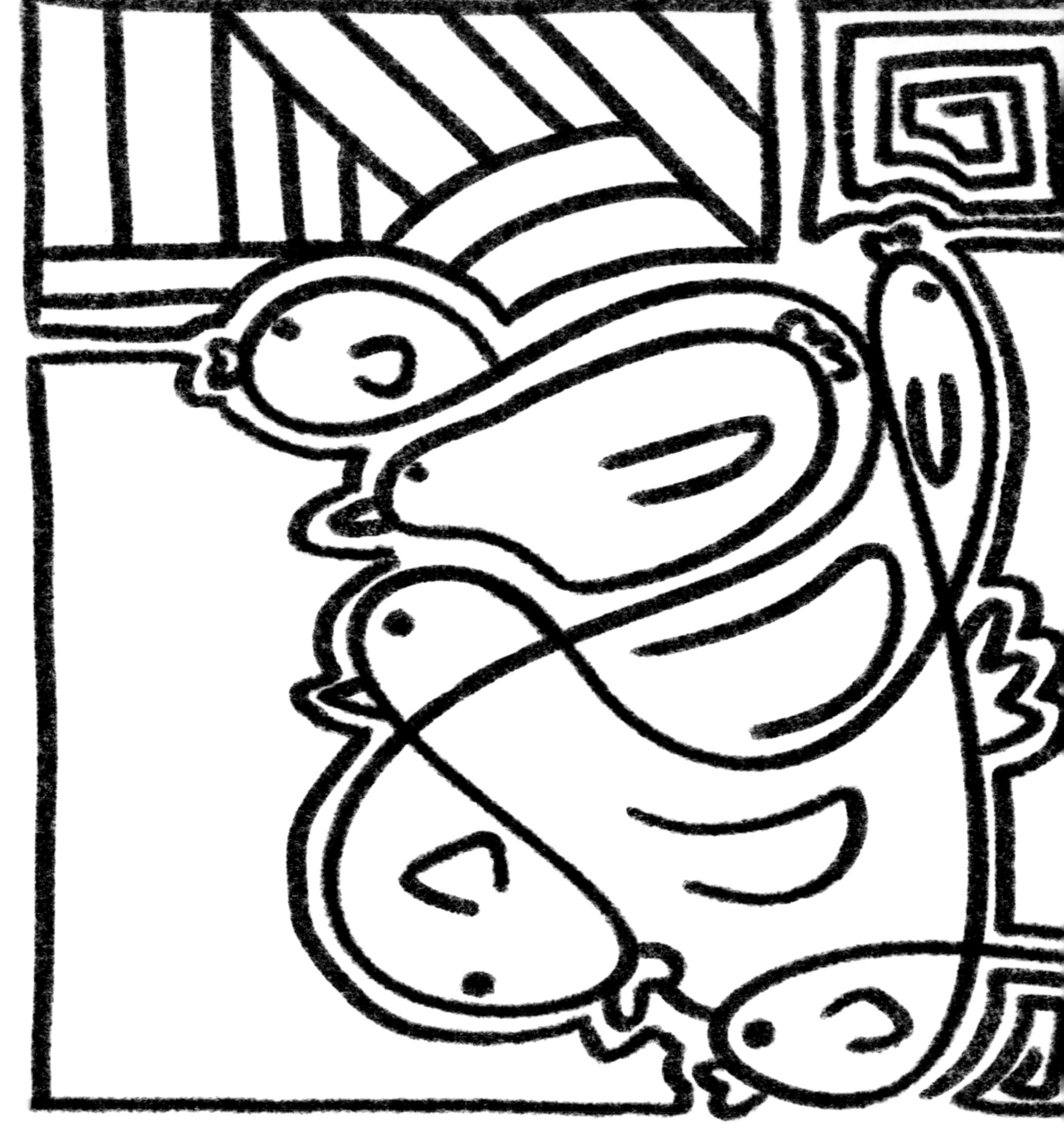

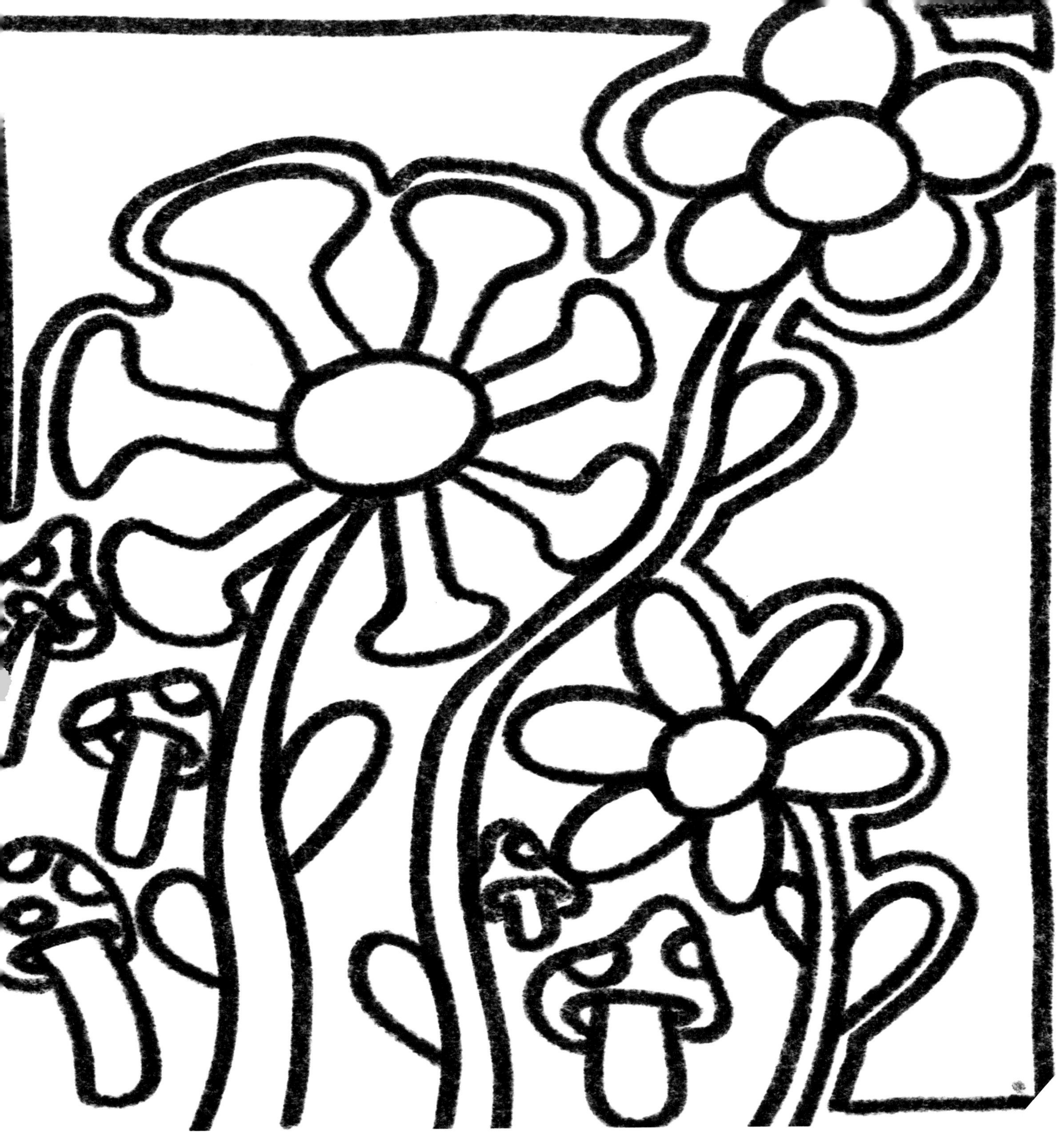

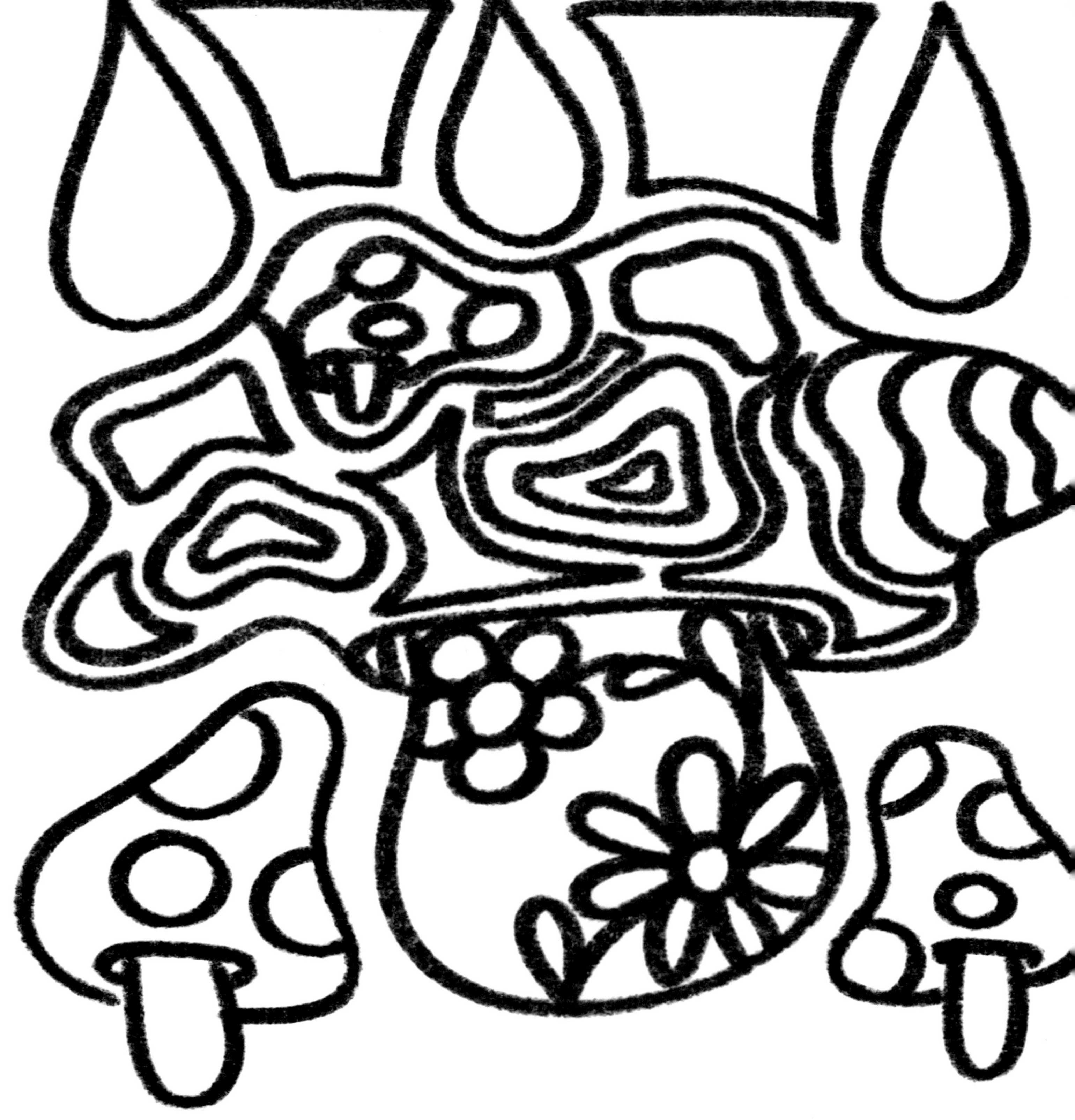

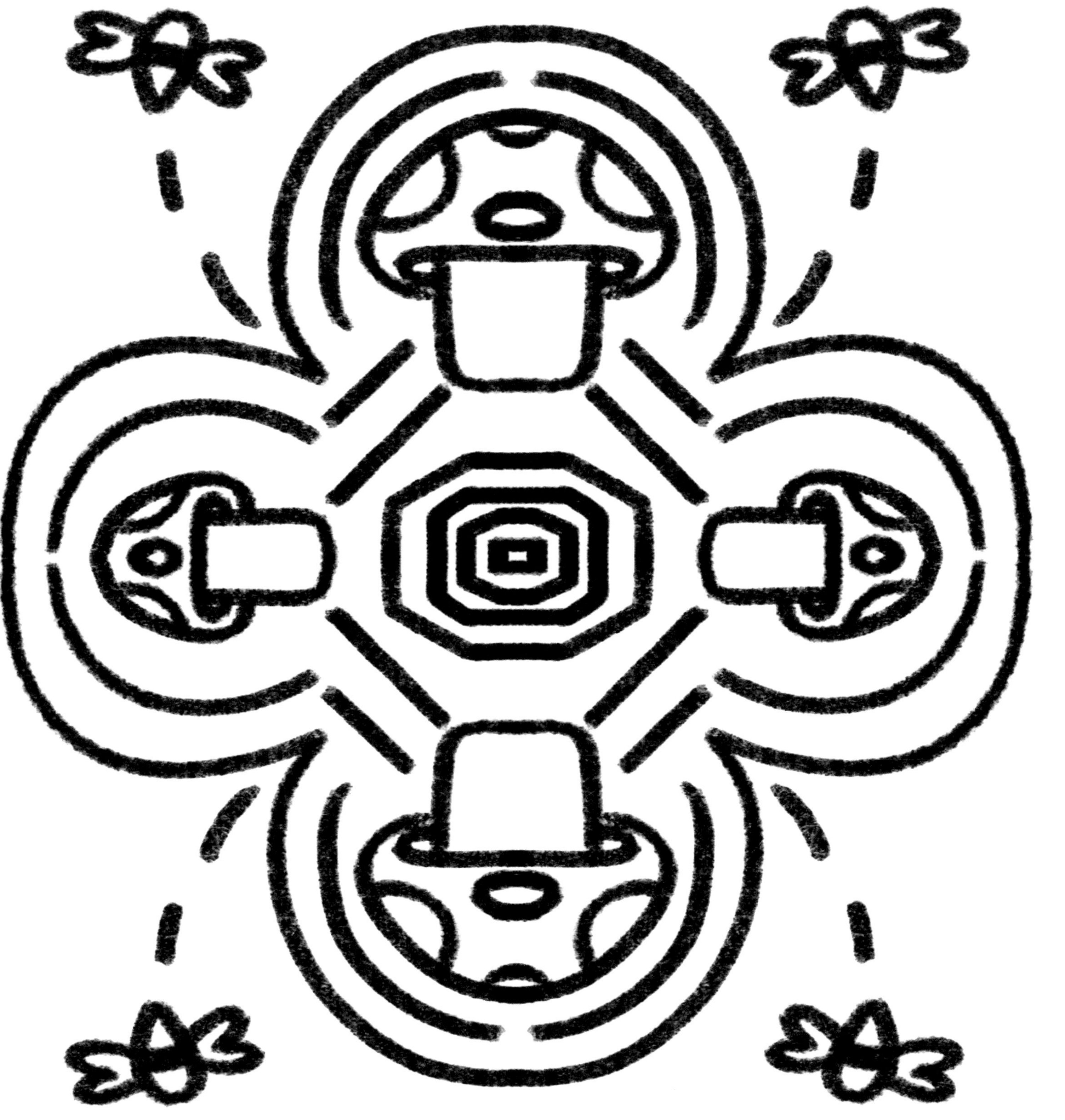

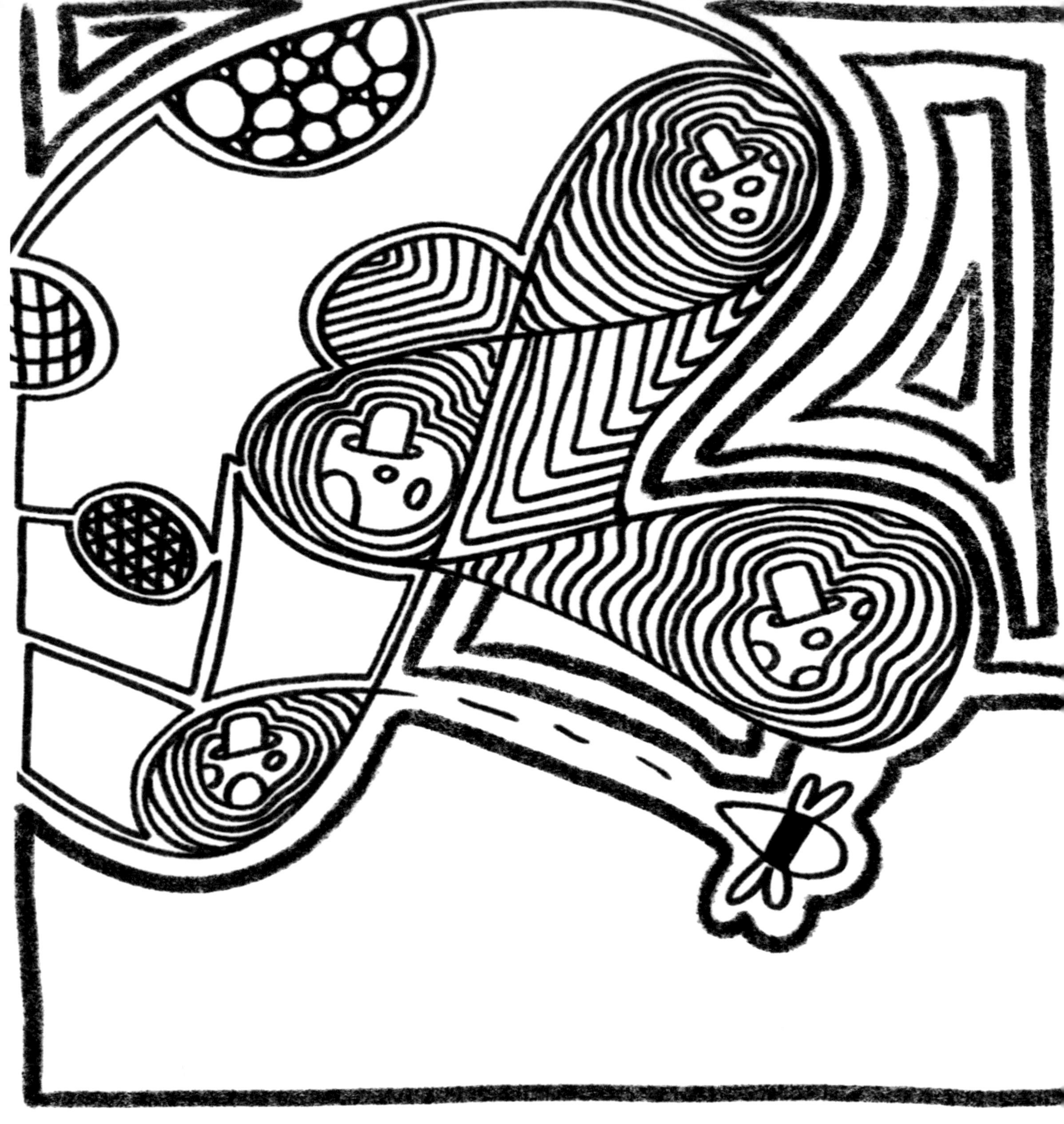